Music

Testimonials

"As soon as I saw the sentence, "allow your heart to guide you," I knew Melody's words contained the truth about life. I say, "When you let your heart make up your mind, magic happens," because as a physician I have seen the benefits of living in your heart versus thinking with your brain. When you live in your heart, you get tired and you may be burning up, but you won't burn out. Read Melody's book and learn the lessons of life the easy way; from her wisdom and not your pain."

-**Dr. Bernie Siegel, MD.**, Author of *Love, Medicine and Miracles, Peace, Love and Healing* and *365 Prescriptions for the Soul*. New York Times bestselling author. Originated "Exceptional Cancer Patients" therapy. www.berniesiegelmd.com

"More often than not, we have to look inside ourselves and do a bit of soul-searching to find answers to the innumerable questions that we have. Melody's brilliant life-changing book caused me to do just that. In doing so, I found reserves of positivity within myself on my path of positive social impact through music. *Heart-Dreamer* is not just a book, it is a way of life."

-**Ricky Kej**, Grammy Award Winning Composer. Conservationist. United Nations "Global Humanitarian Artist." Ambassador to UNESCO MGIEP, UNICEF and the Earth Day Network. www.rickykej.com

"I loved reading *Heart-Dreamer*. It is such a beautiful reflection of the wisdom, light and love that Melody brings to her music and to her life. *Heart-Dreamer* invites me to be gentle with myself and with everyone around me. At the same time, Melody challenges me to dare to dream big. Melody brings a wonderfully personal touch, lifting up her own struggles and foibles with grace and humor. She honors the reality of deep pain without being weighed down by it. I especially appreciate her vivid and sometimes hilarious description of the "noisy voices" that can inhabit our psyches. I resonated with every one of the inner dialogue scripts she describes. Thank you, Melody, for a beautiful and powerful book."

-**Rev. Dr. Deborah L. Clark**, Author of *Ice Cream at the Ashram: Holy Journey, Holy River, Holy Week*. Multi-Faith Coordinator for Open Spirit. Pastor at Edwards Church, UCC. Yoga instructor. www.openspiritcenter.org

"*Heart-Dreamer* is the perfect book for anyone who could use a boost in self-compassion and a stronger connection to their intuition and creativity. The exercises were helpful for focusing my vision and inspiring my next steps on the path. Her stories, told with such honesty and vulnerability, gave me permission to shine my truth more brightly. Melody is a wise and generous cheerleader for the spirit and of the heart."

-**Elisa Pearmain,** LMHC, Psychotherapist. Author of *Doorways to the Soul* and *Once Upon a Time-Storytelling to Teach and Prevent Bullying*. Award-winning album-*Forgiveness: Telling Our Stories in New Ways*. Professional Storyteller. Certified Mindfulness instructor. www.wisdomtales.com

"An intimate workshop of hope and love await you between the pages. Melody's ability to see us singular humans and envision our greatness is a miracle in and of itself. Melody is a creative force of nature! In my profession, the general reader welcomes a writer with such honesty."

-**Ann Marie Speicher,** Reference Librarian, Reader's Adviser, Educator and Editor. www.amspeicher.weebly.com

"The inspiring way that Melody created the book from her own stories to the stories of other people is a gift. *Heart-Dreamer* is a heartfelt inner guide filled with wisdom to help us navigate life's challenges and to live fully alive. From her childhood memories, to her self-discovery process, to her leap of faith towards living her life of dreams, Melody lights up our lives and gives us the courage to follow our dreams."

-**Dot Walsh,** Author of *Finding Light in the Darkness*. Social Justice Activist. Peace Chaplain. Producer and host of "Oneness and Wellness." www.dotwalsh.com, www.onenessandwellness.com

"This is an amazing journey that welcomes the reader with joy, generosity and wisdom. With the support of Melody's thoughtful guidance, each of the chapters is an invitation to explore all your dreams and possibilities. *Heart-Dreamer* opens new doors to everyone, including and especially the one in the mirror."

-**Alan O'Hare,** Author of *Love Mary B: A Teacher's Gift*. Seanchie: Storyteller from the Ancient Celtic tradition. Founder of Life Story Theatre. University Educator. Playwright. www.lifestorytheatre.org

Heart-Dreamer

Stepping into Life, Love, Creativity and Dreams

No Matter What

CHERYL MELODY BASKIN

Book cover design & Ebook conversion by YellowStudios

Library of Congress Cataloging-in-Publication Data
Library of Congress Control Number: 2021915916
Baskin, Cheryl Melody
Heart-Dreamer: Stepping into Life, Love, Creativity and Dreams-No Matter What
Cheryl Melody Baskin
Paperback ISBN 978-1-7333681-7-9

Second Edition

Categories: Non-fiction/Self-Help Personal Growth Happiness Inspiration Memoir/Biography

Published by
Cheryl Melody Baskin, LLC
Boston, Massachusetts
www.CherylMelody.com

To all the heart-dreamers

on our small precious planet.

Thank you.

Contents

A Heart-Dreamer's Welcome

Dreams are a lifeline to hope.

♥

Dear Friend,

Thank you for inviting "Heart-Dreamer" into your life. I am one of "those people" who believes that there is a higher reason for everything. There is a reason that this book came through me, and there is a reason that you were drawn to it. I believe that we met because we are kindred spirits. In our deepest core, we are both heart-dreamers.

Heart-Dreamers look up at the stars with dreams in their eyes, trust in the magical mystery of the unknown, honor their truth, and embrace life with love, courage and curiosity. When a creative idea flashes through their mind, they open their heart, pay attention and listen. They know that creativity is a gift, and they call this gift a magical "wisdom-whisper."

"Heart-Dreamer" was my wisdom-whisper. I heard an inner voice saying, "Hurry! Write this book. Don't procrastinate. The time is now." She was adamant. Why couldn't it wait? My age. One day I woke up and turned seventy-two-years-old.

"Grandmother Time" is giving me a bad headache. With her incessantly loud ticking sounds, she's pointing directly at me and telling me that I better say what I want to say before it's too late.

This is more than a book "all about me." "Heart-Dreamer" overflows with encouragement, unconditional love and abundant experiential opportunities. I've also taken the liberty of dubbing myself your pep talk coach. You see, I'm taking advantage of the age card and the saying, "I'm old and wise. Listen to me." I'm here to give you a gentle nudge that says, "You can do it. Never give up. One step at a time. Patience. Trust. Take a leap of faith. Move forward. Step into your butterfly spirit. Soar with life's infinite possibilities."

♥ *An Invitation:* Step into your dreams. Dreams are a lifeline to hope. When we have our dreams, we have all the food that we need to nurture our spirit towards light. Every day, I turn to my inner heart-dreamer for inspiration, direction, sustenance and hope. She helps me understand the silver lining behind my struggles and the higher meaning behind my life's work. Most of all, she encourages me to believe in myself and to follow my heart.

I walk the path of a heart-dreamer and I would love for you to join me. Let's stand proudly on that metaphorical mountaintop. Let's dance in our light and exclaim to the stars...

I am a heart-dreamer! I stand here with my arms open to all of life's unlimited possibilities! I dream. I act upon my dreams. I love. I am loved. I honor the truth of who I am. I follow the whispers of my heart and walk towards life, love, creativity and dreams, no matter what!

From my heart to yours,

Melody

Setting the Stage

"Every great dream begins with a dreamer. Always remember, you have within you the strength, the patience, and the passion to reach for the stars to change the world."

Harriet Tubman

Heart-Dreamer is meant for everyone. All ages, stages, genders, ethnicities and religions. All people. It is for anyone who has a dream, lost their dreams along the way, or never knew how to dream. Every page is here to inspire you to keep moving forward with light and hope in your heart.

Although there are many layers to this book of wisdom, I didn't want it to be the longest self-help book in history. The content is deep, but to the point. Here are just a few of the highlights.

In "Welcoming Your Creative Muse," each experiential activity is designed to inspire playfulness, imagination, intuition and creative flow.

"A Leap of Faith" focuses on the themes of self-belief, trust and life's mystery.

"Secrets of a Heart-Dreamer" is one of my favorite chapters. It answers the question, "What do magic wands, toddlers, creativity, caution, risk, daydreaming, inner witnessing, self-discovery and love have in common?"

In "Nerve-Busting" and "Overpowering the Inner Critic," I share my techniques and philosophy for overcoming anxiety and self-doubt.

"The Heart of True Success" and "Follow your Heart" inspire us to walk the path of love and peace, no matter what.

"I am Enough," "Best Friends Forever" and "The Healing Poetry of Love" reinforce the importance of self-acceptance and self-love.

"Ebb and Flow" encourages us to dance more gracefully with all the ups and downs of life.

"Chaos in Paradise" and "A Blanket of Love" are deeply personal stories that contain messages for everyone.

In "Community Wisdom," we are joined by new voices of inspiration. Members of the on-line group, "Shift of Heart," share their honest life experiences, perceptive insights and deep wisdom.

Heart-Dreamer is a "read, feel, think, do and become" kind of book and there are no "right" ways to approach it. Experiment. Start at the beginning, dive into the experiential exercises, write your new insights down in a journal, head right for the end, focus on a specific theme, or place the book by your bed and open it to any page that is "meant to be."

As you begin your journey into *Heart-Dreamer*, allow your heart to guide you.

- Chapter One -

Seeds of Inspiration

Everyone we meet along the way becomes
our seed of inspiration.
Yes, even the people that hurt us.
Especially them.
They teach us how not to be.

Please Call Me Melody

"What's in a name?
That which we call a rose by any other name
would smell as sweet."

William Shakespeare

First, allow me to introduce myself. I'll begin with the basics. My name. It may sound like an easy topic to address, but my name has been a complicated subject every day of my life. My full name is Cheryl Melody Baskin Rosenbloom, but don't worry. I'll only talk about my first name.

When I was young, my family called me *Zissy*. It's a Yiddish name and it means "sweet" in English. It is also the name of a deceased family member. Although I appreciated knowing the sentimental reason behind why my family called me "Zissy," whenever I heard it, I shuddered. I knew that it would lead to my being a target of neighborhood bullying. When it was time for me to come home from playing outside, I winced every time I heard my mom yelling, *"ZISSY! Time for dinner!"* If it had been possible to dissolve into the ground like the wicked witch in the *Wizard of Oz*, I would have gladly obliged. She tried to lighten up the name by changing it to the softer sound of *Zisseleh*, but the newer version didn't help me out at all. I felt like disappearing even more.

My name is also *Cheryl*. It's a beautiful name, I like it much better than Zissy, but it never feels like *my* name. I don't know why. All I know is that it doesn't seem like the *real* me and I feel detached from it.

Luckily, I've had many other first names pop up along the way…

My dad enjoyed calling me *Chéri* and he always said it with a French accent that felt loving and playful. I think he knew that I didn't like my other names and created a new one to help me feel better.

When I studied music in college, some of my friends liked to call me *Sherry.* Coincidentally, the most popular song on the radio was "Sherry Baby." As soon as my friends noticed me walking down the hall with my cello, they loved to run in front of me and sing me their latest personalized rendition. Their playful interaction began when I was a freshman and continued through my senior year. Imagine. Four long years of "Sherry Baby."

Some of my sweet family and friends call me *Cher* instead of Cheryl. It sounds like *Cheryl, Chéri* and *Sherry,* but not quite. It's friendly and I like it.

When I need an extra dose of inner strength and courage, I secretly call myself *Cheyenne.* I breathe in the healing vibration of Sedona and imagine the essence of myself as Cheyenne. She is a dreamer who walks confidently on the sacred earth with fierce determination and bold resilience. With every step, she is unstoppable, persistent, loving and strong.

As a performing artist and educator, everyone knows me as *Cheryl Melody.* When I hear my young students call me Cheryl Melody, it brings a smile to my face and joy to my heart.

My grandchildren spontaneously dubbed me *Grelody.* It's a combination of Grandma and Melody. I love it.

My middle name is *Melody,* and several years ago I claimed it as my first name. *Melody is the ME of me. It is my spirit, my heart and who I am.* My soul recognizes its vibration of love, music, wisdom, imagination, courage and dreams. When someone calls me Melody, my spirit feels visible, understood, loved and respected. I say to myself, "Yes. Here I am. Thank you my friend. Thank you for calling me Melody."

As I gain deeper insight into my past, my goal is to be at peace with all my names and with all parts of myself. Each name has led me to my true "spirit name." I am Zissy, Zisseleh, Cheryl, Sherry, Cheryl Melody, Chéri, Cher and Cheyenne, (and a few other names that I didn't mention), but most of all, please call me...

MELODY!

What's Your Name?

"Ever since happiness heard your name, it has been running through the streets calling your name."

Hafez

Now that I've shared many of my first names and all the complicated emotions surrounding them, I'm curious. How do you feel about your first name? Do you like it? Does it feel like the real you? Does it project the essence of who you really are?

If you feel emotionally distant from your first name, consider dubbing yourself with a new one. Which name would you choose for yourself today? Just for a few minutes, allow your imagination to run free. Of all the names in the world, which one speaks to your personality, talents, visions, goals and dreams? Is there a name that speaks to your heart and feels more like the *real* you?

In many traditions, this special name is called a "spirit name," "imagination name" or "vibrational name."

If you decide to anoint yourself with a new name, don't worry about anything. You don't need to go through any paperwork and change it legally, and you don't need to force resistant family and friends to change their normal way of referring to you. Let go of any expectations and just smile to yourself. *You* know your true spirit name and that's all that matters.

Because life is growth and change, there may come a time when the spirit name that you chose no longer fits you. The solution is simple. Create a new one.

Free yourself to be yourself. This is your life.

Your spirit name is a sacred vibration and there are many ways to use it. You can keep it a delightful secret and only use it when you talk to yourself. You can also use it as a catalyst for shedding distasteful parts of your past or for elevating your present and future.

Your spirit name symbolizes new beginnings.

The most comfortable time to step into your new name is when you meet new people. Be bold. Claim your sacred name and stand tall in its high vibration. In Native American tradition, spirit names are known to carry magical powers. Invite these powers into your life every minute of your day.

Whichever name you choose,
it's very nice to meet you.

Sticks, Stones and Words

I couldn't understand intolerance when I was seven-years-old,
and it is still impossible for me to understand intolerance
at seventy-two-years-old.

This is a glimpse into my life as a young girl…

My roots are Jewish, and when I was young, religious prejudice led to my being the target of cruel jokes, teasing, bullying, isolation and physical aggression. Although fear and anxiety were a large part of my inner life, I never told my family about my everyday challenges in the neighborhood. For some reason, I wanted to protect them. On the surface, I seemed "fine." I was a good student, quietly followed all the rules and acted relatively "normal." Deep down, I wasn't fine.

"Sticks and stones can break my bones, but words can also break me."

Despite these challenges, I was lucky. I had a good family. While my parents worked, my grandmother, whom we called "bubby," took care of me. I still smile at the memories of the two of us together. I remember her strong personality, playful sense of humor, beautiful singing voice, and her ability to tell spellbinding stories about her past. I also remember every swear word that she taught me in Yiddish and the many good laughs that followed. She was as spunky as they come.

In the 1950's, everyone left school for an hour to go home for lunch. I went to bubby's house. After I devoured her delicious homemade potato pancakes, we watched the newest episode of the soap opera, *Love of Life*. As the drama unfolded, we sighed, groaned, moaned and laughed together. It was fun and I would have given anything to stay in my comfortable cocoon of safety forever. Unfortunately, it wasn't meant to be. All too soon, it was time to go back to school for the rest of the afternoon.

As I left, Bubby took ten cents out of her piggy bank and placed it into my hands. She winked at me and whispered, "Don't tell your mother. Stop at the corner store and buy yourself a little candy."

The choice between Sugar Daddies, Cracker Jacks, Ludden's Cherry Cough Drops, Red Wax Lips, Red Hot Fireballs, Taffy, Bubble Gum, Tootsie Rolls, Candy Necklaces, Sugar Babies or Pixy Stix was quite challenging for my sweet tooth. Once I made my final decisions, I carried the bag of candy to school and placed it inside my desk.

Several hours later, I got into trouble.

My teacher turned her back, I gave my peers all my candy, and in one moment of glory, I became the most popular second grader of all time. I wasn't as popular with the adult crowd, however. They let me know that they were deeply disappointed and extremely embarrassed by my behavior. The teacher was shocked, my parents punished me, and the school principal called me into the office and smacked my bottom with her oversized orange paddle.

I'd like to save face and tell you that my behavior was motivated by generosity. In truth, it was a desperate survival tool and a cry for help. I used a sweet path to bribe the kids to stop bullying me. On the surface, my behavior was cute and innocuous. Under the surface, I was a terrified and isolated child who longed for acceptance.

I couldn't understand intolerance when I was seven-years-old, and it is still impossible for me to understand intolerance at seventy-two-years-old. If my family hadn't shown me the power of love, my childhood would have been unbearable.

My mom was an endless source of inspiration. She was a gifted opera singer, actress and writer, and because of her passion for the arts, she urged me to step into my own talents as well. Even when we clashed, our mutual interest in music always returned us back to the center of love. I was her number one fan and she was mine.

Even at the end of her life, music continued to be our special bond...

I remember sitting by her bed. Her eyes were closed and her breathing was labored. Suddenly she opened her eyes, adamantly pointed to my guitar, and then closed her eyes again. I quickly grabbed my guitar and sang one of her favorite Hebrew songs of hope, "Hinei Mah Tov." *How good and pleasant it is for people to dwell together in unity.* And there we were. Mother and daughter. In unity.

As I sat by her bed and continued to sing, I found it unbearable to think that I would never hear her voice again. Then, a miracle happened. She opened her eyes and began to harmonize with me. Her mezzo soprano voice soared beyond the walls of the room and it sounded stronger than ever. When she felt a sense of completion, she gently closed her eyes again. The healing power of music and love graced us with a six-minute musical goodbye. With my sister and I surrounding her with light and love, she died six days later. On my birthday.

My dad was equally inspirational. He was loving, hardworking and gifted. He designed and sold jewelry, thrived on being a small business entrepreneur, and challenged his mind by taking adult education classes. He also enjoyed traveling, participated in deep philosophical discussions, wrote poetry, and created rhyming jingles for every one of my birthday cards.

He had a comedic side too. He got a kick out of sharing the silly jokes, jingles and songs that he remembered from his childhood. It didn't matter how many times my younger sister and I heard one of his jokes, we laughed every single time. I can still hear him. "You look good! Who's your undertaker?" "What time is It? Half-past a freckle!" When he couldn't figure out an answer to a problem, he would utter his nonsense word, "Moskamadehtu."

Most of all, my dad taught me to keep a twinkle in my eyes and to live life to the fullest. And do you know how he died? Dancing. Now that's the way to do it.

If my family hadn't been as loving as they were, what would have happened to me? Would I have made bad choices? Had a chip on my shoulder? Given up on life?

♥ **Life Wisdom:** I think about you and your life too. Why were you drawn to *Heart-Dreamer*? Who were your seeds of inspiration? Did you need to light your own way? Were your childhood experiences more emotionally challenging than mine? If so, you are the strong one my friend. I applaud and admire your steadfast determination, courage and strength. Thank you for being here and fighting for yourself. Thank you for caring enough about yourself to make it through anything and everything.

"No matter how painful your young memories are, there were also glorious moments that kept you alive or you would not be here today."

Sarah Ban Breathnach

Everyone we meet along the way becomes our seed of inspiration. Yes, even the people that hurt us. Especially them. They teach us how *not* to be. Stand proudly in your colorful fabric of resilience. Never let your vision of a better future dissipate. The depth of your life stories, your unique personality, brilliant survival skills and persistent spirit are all qualities of pure beauty. Deep inside your spirit, you have the skill and desire to heal your past, empower your present, and create a positive and hopeful future.

Despite what you have gone through,

hold your head high

and keep your dreams coming.

Just One Person

"To love someone is to learn the song in their heart and sing it to them when they have forgotten it."

Arne Garborg

When I was fifteen, my family introduced me to Morris. He was a physician, philosopher, mystic and poet and I felt drawn towards his wisdom. I remember the day when we had a deep talk that changed my life forever. Morris took me under his wing and saw me as an old soul who had depth. He encouraged me to honor my introspective nature, and he supported my desire to write, sing, create and dream. In fact, Morris adamantly *insisted* that I offer my attributes to the world.

He would say, "You have been blessed with many talents my friend. It is your *responsibility* to share them. Don't hide. Carve your unique imprint. Give back. This is the only way to reflect a spiritual *thank you* to the universe for all the gifts that you have been given."

If Morris and I hadn't connected as deeply, would I have felt like a lost soul forever? If we hadn't met, would I have pursued a rich creative life? Would I have listened to the whispers and wisdom of my heart as often as I do now? It's hard to know the answers, but I am confident that his strong influence, loving push and deep wisdom made a profound impact on the trajectory of my life.

♥ **Life Wisdom:** What about your own life? Were you graced with people who believed in you? Did you feel seen, heard and loved? Did someone see more light in you than you saw in yourself? I hope that you were one of the lucky ones who received all the support that you needed to thrive. If you didn't meet an inspiring person like Morris, and if nobody gave you their guiding hand, wisdom and heart, I have an idea. To offset any of your private moments of sadness, anger and regret, become someone's mentor. You have the power to shift your painful memories into opportunities towards personal growth and healing. You know how it feels when there is no one around to encourage you.

Shift those negative feelings into a spark towards positive change, altruism, healing and hope.

When you become the light that inspires others, your own spirit heals too. Everyone needs a light-worker. Look at the impact Morris made to just one life. Mine. His deep wisdom and listening heart were like medicine for my lost soul.

Encourage someone's sunflower spirit

to grow into their full potential.

BE that gift. ONE person can become

a positive force to ONE life.

Solitude and Community

"Every artist dips his brush in his own soul
and paints his own nature into his pictures."

Henry Ward Beecher

Which word defines your basic personality? Are you an extrovert or an introvert? Because I don't fit into either category, I always wondered if there was something "wrong" with me. Luckily, I discovered the perfect definition for my quirky personality. I am an ambivert. An ambivert is both an introvert and an extrovert and I am happy to announce that society considers me perfectly "normal."

I savor my solitude, am stimulated by deep interpersonal connection, delight in superficial chitchat, and enjoy endless hours of over-the-top daydreaming. My moments of surface chitchat involve the daily weather report. Because I am a wannabe meteorologist, I enjoy sharing the latest hourly report with anyone who has the attention span to listen. I think Winnie the Pooh started it all when he told Christopher Robin, "Tut-tut, it looks like rain."

My over-the-top daydream centers around the Academy Awards at the Dolby Theatre in Hollywood. I love the Oscars. Don't laugh, but sometimes I dress in a formal evening gown to watch it. Then, I begin to daydream...

Next year, what if one of the award-winning actors invites me to attend the Oscars in person? Let's see. Who will invite me? Meryl Steep? Nicole Kidman? Denzel Washington? Bradley Cooper? There I am on the red carpet wearing one of my many custom-made gowns and looking ever-so poised and radiant. After the Award ceremony ends, I return to my beautiful home on my island of paradise. Ahh. Until next year everyone.

Despite my propensity to daydream, I have always needed more depth and substance. For as long as I can remember, I craved a connection with people who were willing to exchange honest life experiences, lessons learned, raw emotions, coping tools and personal dreams. I yearned to find similar souls who believed in a "one planet of love, peace and hope" philosophy. One day it happened. I created an on-line community of likeminded people and gave the group the same name as the title of my first book, *Shift of Heart-Paths to Healing and Love.*

Its philosophy is love. Inclusive, supportive and respectful. We form a circle of healing light around those in need, provide a space for confidential conversations, and honor each person's unique voice. To offer the community further inspiration, I create videos with life coaching pep talks. When my "Shift of Heart" members tell me that my words were "just what they needed to hear," I am humbled by their feedback. It reminds me of Morris and what he told me when I was fifteen. "Give back. It is the only way to offer a spiritual *thank you* to the universe for all the gifts that you have been given."

When I first created the "Shift of Heart" community, I was clear about my mission. I would lead, inspire, listen, support and guide its members. They would be part of my global family and I would treat each person with love and respect. Although my intention was to support them in every way that I could, my own life suddenly turned upside down and I was the one who needed *their* support. Without this community, I wouldn't have had the strength to make it through an extremely tough time. I shifted away from being a "loner," and in the chapter "Ebb and Flow," I share the dramatic events that motivated me to change my attitude.

I honor all parts of my personality. I enjoy the solitude of my own company, cherish my family and friends, and value the "Shift of Heart" community. I am a proud ambivert.

Balance your own life between solitude and human connection. Expand your circle of love and support. Imagine a multitude of people applauding you, and when you feel weak, they remind you of your strength.

You can do it. You're stronger than you think.

Trust. Follow your heart.

We're with you all the way.

Stand Proud!

(From the album, "Celebrate" by Cheryl Melody ©)

"My story is the story of thousands of children from around the world. I hope it inspires others to stand up for their rights."

Malala Yousafzai

Stand up stand up, stand up for yourself
Claim your shining star
Rise up rise up, proud of yourself
Please tell us who you are.

Where do you come from? Please make us aware
Who are you? Let your heart sing
Take off your mask, your history share
What pain and joy do you bring?

All kinds of prejudice came to me
But it won't eat me away
For with this pain, I have set myself free
And that's who I am today.

We are one family after all
We smile, bleed and breathe the same way
Red, yellow, black or white, short or tall
Take off your mask today.

Stand up stand up, stand up for yourself
You are beautiful as can be
Rise up rise up, proud of yourself
And set our one family free.

- Chapter Two -

Healing from Inside Out

Never give up.
When you least expect it,
life will shift for the better.
You will experience light on your face
and hope in your heart.
Trust.
Every moment is an opportunity for rebirth.

Vegetables or Desserts?

Warning. This chapter may make you hungry.

♥

As I wrote the chapter, "Healing from Inside-Out," I tossed and turned and struggled…

What a writer's dilemma! Should I place "Healing from Inside-Out" towards the end of the book? After all, this chapter is more experiential, instructional and less "romantic" than the others. Should the more philosophical and creative chapters be placed in the beginning? When should I give my readers all my delicious "desserts?" What if they feel the need to revive their inner dreamer as quickly as possible?

As you can tell, I am one of those people who has the "disease to please," but after focused contemplation, I am at peace with my final decision. "Healing from Inside-Out" is the foundation and backbone of *Heart-Dreamer* and it needs to be the second chapter. When we work on healing ourselves from inside-out, our personal and professional lives become increasingly congruent and our journey towards manifesting our dreams feels ultimately more enjoyable. My decision reminds me of an old motto. "Eat your vegetables first. We'll enjoy all the delicious desserts later."

I look at this chapter as a smorgasbord of healthy and healing spiritual vegetables. When I was in my thirties, my soul craved them. I read motivational self-help books, sought out inspiring mentors, and participated in workshops on transformational change. Forty years later, I am still an openminded and willing student.

In fact, I applied meditation, journal writing, visualization and positive affirmations to help me write the content of *Heart-Dreamer*. Each approach provided me with soul-searching questions…

Underneath the roles and labels of wife, mother, grandmother, daughter, sister, aunt, cousin, friend, writer, peace dreamer, educator and musician, who am I? What are my "pearls of wisdom?" What have I learned about creativity, dreams, taking a leap of faith, listening to the wisdom-whispers, intuition, heart-listening, inner peace, love and healing? What are my personal challenges and inner obstacles? Which transformational tools help me transcend these inner challenges and obstacles? What can I say to motivate my readers to dance towards light, hope and dreams, no matter what?

I also weave these healing tools into my everyday life. I reach for "inside-out" techniques that teach me how to live with joy *and* chaos, strength *and* weakness, light *and* darkness. Each transformational gem offers me a spiritual tonic towards self-understanding, inner peace and love.

♥ **Life Wisdom:** In a way, these techniques are not just healthy and healing spiritual vegetables. They are also soothing and delicious desserts. Do you remember that famous line from *Forest Gump* about life and a box of chocolates?

Here is another metaphor. Treat yourself like the whole blueberry pie. Now that I've got you thinking about blueberry pie and how you would really prefer to eat cherry or apple, let me explain. Have you ever had these thoughts?

When all my dreams come true, then I'll be happy. When I'm rich and fa-mous, then I'll be happy. When I get well again, then I'll be happy. When I don't have to work anymore, then I'll be happy. When I get a job, then I'll be happy. When I find the right partner, then I'll be happy. When I end this relationship, then I'll be happy. When I have more friends, then I'll be happy. When I can get some peace and quiet around here, then I'll be happy.

Our "if only" list goes on and on, doesn't it? While many of these "if only" goals may sound like a key to a great life, true happiness and in-ner peace are really "inside-out" jobs. Our body, mind and spirit dance as one holistic unit and each part seeks to work in harmony with each other. Let's tune ourselves up and live like the whole blueberry pie, or as the saying goes, like the whole enchilada.

You've probably heard stories about successful people who ultimately sabotaged and destroyed their lives. Despite talent, glitter and accolades, they lost their way. They forgot about the importance of love and all the inner qualities that really matter. When it's time to make our own personal and professional life choices, we don't want to do anything that sabotages and destroys us.

> ***Always follow your heart towards the center of love. Self-discovery, inner growth, healing, dream-making and love all dance on the same path together.***

Healing and transformation are on-going adventures and I continue to learn what I continue to teach. Because I am an imperfect human being doing the best I can, I reach for any healthy approach that can make my life easier. To make your own life easier, explore these healing tools too. Like potato chips, once you have tasted a few delicious enticements, it will be hard to stop yourself from wanting more. The path towards self-discovery and inner healing take courage, and I am in your corner rooting for you all the way. I am confident that you have the inner resolve to become much more than your negative thoughts, feelings and experiences. Something inside your spirit led you to pick up *Heart-Dreamer* and it speaks volumes about your passionate desire to grow, heal, create and dream. Use all the tools in "Healing from Inside-Out" to help guide you towards living your one life with light in your heart, freedom in your soul and dreams in your eyes. Be patient with yourself. Inner growth takes a lifetime.

As I say to my children, "The only way to begin is to begin."

First Things First

"The fact that I can plant a seed and it becomes a flower, share a bit of knowledge and it becomes another's, smile at someone and receive a smile in return, are to me continual spiritual exercises."

Leo Buscaglia, PhD

♥

Before we dive into anything "fancy," let's explore four basic tools for inner healing and self-discovery…

A Journal: In her book, *Write On! How to Make Writing a Pleasurable Pastime,* Irene Hannigan says, "I continue to think that journal entries are a legitimate form of writing to share. Often an entry, or even an excerpt will illuminate an observation or a feeling or an insight that actually does mean something of consequence for the writer."

When you write in your journal, allow all your feelings to flow from inside-out. Don't worry about the correct spelling, grammar, punctuation and sentence structure. Just let it rip. Stream of consciousness. If you don't own a journal, go to your favorite bookstore and notice all the covers, the way each one opens, the lines or no lines, and the shapes and sizes. You'll know when you have spotted just the right one.

An Empathic Friend: Choose your friends wisely. An empathic friend is fully present, listens to you with a compassionate heart, openly shares their weaknesses and strengths, and is loving, supportive and non-judgmental. What if you felt safe enough to share all your hopes, dreams, fears and struggles with this friend? What if you felt safe enough to read your sacred journals to each other? I can't think of a more wonderful friendship.

Community: There is nothing as beautiful as people helping people. We are one human family, and when we make a conscious effort to love and support each other, the energetic vibration of the entire planet lifts to a higher frequency. Throughout *Heart-Dreamer*, there are sections called "Community Wisdom." Because I didn't want to be the only voice of wisdom that you heard, the "Shift of Heart" community offers a village of love, wisdom and support.

Reach Out: If you need additional support, seek out a good therapist. Please don't go through this life alone. Fight for yourself. Reach out.

Healing from Inside Out: Patricia is an active member of the "Shift of Heart" community. Here is why she is motivated to heal…

"I am willing to do the hard inner work. I face my fears, grief and anger, and I trust that they will all eventually lift, change and shift. I want to get "my issues out of my tissues!" Despite discomfort, I am willing to feel all my feelings."

Just like Patricia, let's dig in. Let's explore the world of creative visualization, sound healing, meditation, the healing power of words, and the "stop sign technique." Enjoy your own inside-out journey towards self-discovery, transformational healing and meaningful adventure.

Reach out. Grow from within. Heal.

Visualization

In the best and worst of times, it is a spiritual lifeline to imagine hope and possibility. Hopelessness is the worst disease of all.

♥

Visualization is one of my favorite "healing from inside-out" approaches. As soon as I visualize a positive outcome to a difficult problem, my attitude shifts.

Relationships: I use the visualization technique when we are having marital issues. Eventually. After I get over my hurt, anger, stubbornness, self-righteous indignation and frustration. I imagine what it might look like if we were willing to forgive each other and open our hearts to love and understanding. Magically, as soon as I visualize a better relationship, it happens.

A New Day: I know that I'm taking advantage of this magical tool, but I reach for it even before I start my day. I keep my eyes closed longer, linger in bed, stay relaxed, and breathe in the energy of specific power words and images. I see myself greeting the day with an open heart, strength, optimism, clarity, compassion, patience and humor. I know that I'm asking a lot from myself as an imperfect human being, but why not reach for it? If patience and strength allude me that day, perhaps my natural optimism, open heart and humor will shine. If I am willing to take a few minutes in the morning to imagine a day of light and love, every thought, feeling and interaction will be surrounded by conscious and positive energy. Guaranteed.

Daydreaming: I also use this inner tool to imagine and illuminate all my hopes and dreams. Every idea begins as a seed in our imagination. It starts with a daydream and makes itself known in our dreams at night. Remember the movie, *Pinocchio*? When I was little, I loved hearing Jiminy Cricket sing, "When You Wish Upon a Star." The lyrics inspired me to dream even more.

Wow! All the dreams in my heart really CAN come true. I'll just do what Jiminy Cricket told me. I'll keep imagining the impossible, believe in my dreams, and keep wishing on those wishing stars forever.

The Third Eye: The third eye chakra is located between our two eyebrows and it is one of my favorite chakras. Why? It is the center of vibration for our highest intuition and greatest wisdom. If you haven't heard of the third eye before, it may seem like an odd concept at first. Ironically, you probably use your third eye every day without knowing it. Do you ever have a strong hunch and it turns out to be accurate? Do you ever think that your phone will ring and then it does? This is your third eye energy center making itself known to you. I love knowing about this sixth chakra. I am always relieved to think that I can tap into a higher part of myself. The third eye is that gut feeling, but more. It is our intuition, but stronger. When I am open to its transformational energy, I hear my inner voice whisper new ideas, unfolding dreams and creative solutions to problems.

♥ **Life Wisdom:** I know that visualization can't make everything happen magically. Dreams don't always become a reality. When we are ill, we don't always recover. No matter what, I will continue to believe in its power towards healing. In the best and worst of times, it is a spiritual lifeline to imagine hope and possibility. Hopelessness is the worst disease of all.

With every thought, feeling and

interaction, visualize hope.

A Free Vacation

"There are painters who transform the sun to a yellow spot, but there are others who, with the help of their art and their intelligence, transfer a yellow spot into the sun."

Pablo Picasso

Visualization is a muscle that needs consistent exercise. Imagine the following scenes and allow your mind to linger inside each snapshot. Do you crave a mental and emotional vacation? Well, here it is. And the best part about this vacation? It's free. There are no expenses, heavy suitcases, late flights or questionable lodgings.

✳ An Experiential Activity:

- Walk barefoot on the beach at low tide.

- Breathe in the smell of freshly baked bread.

- Touch the bark of a redwood tree.

- Watch a colorful butterfly flutter around the purple and yellow flowers.

- See yourself paddling a yellow and orange kayak on a smooth and glistening lake.

- Eat a mouthwatering dessert.

- Write your name on the sidewalk. Use three different colors of chalk.

- Watch the rising sun.

- Stand on top of a mountain and observe the shifting colors of the sunset.

- Follow a rainbow as long as it takes.

And now for dessert.

Visualize all your hopes and dreams. Let every detail pour from your heart and onto the pages of your sacred journal.

♥ **Life Wisdom:** Visualization is a life-changing tool that can be applied to both our personal and professional lives. For example, Olympic ice skaters use the visualization technique to help them reach their full potential. Before they perform, they find a quiet space, and with focused concentration, place themselves inside the movie of their inner mind. As they mentally review their upcoming performance, they see themselves skating flawlessly. They picture the smoothness of the ice, see the laces on their skates in perfect condition and tied well, notice every clasp on their stunning costume secure, hear the applause of the crowd, skate with the emotional impact of the music, delight in the agility of their body, and most of all, they see themselves accomplishing every flip, spin, toe loop, Lutz, Salchow and Triple Axel with perfection and ease.

Visualization can be applied to countless situations. I use it to send healing energy to those in need, to imagine a better relationship, to invite more positive situations into my life, to hold a space for a peaceful world, before I go on a plane, and for medical procedures. I also apply it to my professional life. Here is a personal story that may convince you of its transformational power.

Many years ago, I was asked to be a featured speaker at a Montessori conference. I wrote my speech, planned my workshop, practiced for weeks, imagined the event going well, and listened endlessly to a guided visualization on *Overcoming Fear*.

It was time to fly to Chicago. My presentation was scheduled for the following morning, and I couldn't wait to offer my heart, music and expertise. I checked into my hotel room, unpacked, took a shower, had a good dinner, socialized, got into my pajamas, reviewed my notes, watched TV, and then suddenly something inside me shifted.

Feelings of intense anxiety and overwhelming panic set into my body. I paced, shivered, sweat and cried. My stomach hurt, I was filled with self-doubt, and I wanted to go home. It appeared as if all the mind rehearsals that I had done at home were not going to work when it really counted.

Despite everything, I was determined to find the strength to overcome it. After all, my deep sense of pride and professional survival were at stake. I remember staying up all night to do the inner work necessary to refocus my mind. I wrote in my journal, created positive affirmations, and visualized a good outcome.

I fought to get myself back on track, no matter what.

Instead of visualizing failure, I imagined what it would feel like if my event went well. Here is a glimpse into my inner dialogue.

I can do this. I have what it takes. I project myself with confidence, energy, authenticity and interactive engagement. I get out of my own way and step into my full potential. My audience feels my heart, expertise and positive intentions. The connection between us is palatable. I am living my dream and am fully present in each moment. I am grateful for this opportunity, and I step into it as if I have done it forever.

It was time. I centered myself, mentally revisited my affirmations and visualizations, smiled at everyone warmly, stepped forward with confidence, and began. The outcome? Believe it or not, I received a standing ovation. Visualization works for me, and it can work for you too.

"The only person you are destined to become is the person you decide to be."

Ralph Waldo Emerson

Clarity, Truth, Strength and Love

Words matter.

I have a favorite affirmation. "I speak my truth with clarity, strength and love." How did it become my mantra? When my mom was in the hospital, I had to "sword fight" with the doctors about the quality of her care. Serious mistakes were being made. I had to do something about it.

The Magic Formula: When I spoke up, I wanted to be careful about my choice of words and the tone in my voice. I didn't want to sound too nice and wimpy. I didn't want to sound too brash and angry. I took a deep breath and conveyed all my messages of truth with "clarity, strength and love." I delivered them with a tone and intention that came from my "power belly," and I delivered them with a tone and intention that came from my heart. After he listened to my point of view, the doctor seemed moved and he nodded in agreement.

Hmm. What happened? Despite warnings to the contrary, speaking up to him was a piece of cake. Was my positive result just a lucky break? What if it hadn't worked out? How would I have handled myself if he had ignored me? Disrespected me? Walked away? Told me off?

♥ **Life Wisdom:** Even when we communicate our feelings respectfully, there are no guarantees that we will receive a positive response in return. That's life in real time, isn't it? When we plan what we are going to say and practice our speech in the mirror, it works every time. In reality, our well-designed and well-intentioned communication may or may not work.

Here are the most useful communication tips that I have discovered along the way…

- Listen with an open heart.

- While you continue to stand in the backbone of your truth, do your best to hear the other person's point of view as well.

- Find a way to shift your mind and heart just a little more.

- Avoid accusations, name calling, impatience, bullying, blame and all "low road" approaches.

- Brainstorm win-win solutions together.

- Be willing to empathize and compromise.

- Speak from a place of love and strength.

- If you find yourself at an impasse, give yourself space. When the timing is right, you'll know what to do.

- Be at peace. You tried your best to communicate with truth, clarity, strength and love.

You can't ask anymore from yourself than doing your best.

Positive Power Words

Positive words propel us into an "I can do anything" attitude.

Visualize the following affirmations as if you are already living them. Write your favorite sentences down on post-it notes or index cards. Place them throughout your home, on your mirrors, in your workplace and in your car. Say them out loud before you go to sleep, when you wake up and throughout your day.

✳ An Experiential Activity:

- I follow the whispers of my heart.

- I will, I can, and I am.

- Yea, me!

- Love is my only path.

- *I* define who I am.

- I have the power to change my life.

- I am my own champion.

- I give *myself* permission.

- I stand up for myself.

- I matter.

- I claim my full space in the world.

- I am enough.

- I am courageous, determined and strong.

- I speak my truth with clarity, strength and love.

- I listen to the voice of my highest intuition.

- I am my own best friend.

- I show up for myself.

- I've got this.

- I let go of the past, focus on the present, and keep moving forward.

- All good flows my way.

♥ **Life Wisdom:** Positive affirmations feed the subconscious a different story. A better story. They are designed to be empowering and life-changing, and if we say them often enough, we learn to live them as our truth.

When you design your affirmations, eliminate unhelpful words like can't, should, could, try, wish, soon, maybe, if, hopefully, when, won't, never, not and will. They contain negative energy and reinforce feelings of insecurity, hopelessness and fear. If we say, "I won't be afraid," it feels different to me than saying, "I am courageous." Both sentences have the same intention, but "afraid" and "won't" are loaded with negativity.

The formula for creating effective affirmations and visualizations is simple. Keep them positive. If we say, "I can't do this," then we can't. If we say, "I can do this," then we will, we can, and we are. If we think that we're going to have a bad day, then we will. If we imagine a good day, all kinds of wonderful people and situations show up for us.

Of course, there is a caveat. Even if we design the most beautiful affirmations in the world, there are no guarantees that our lives will run smoothly. What we *can* control is what we tell ourselves. Let's tell ourselves healthier stories and offer ourselves better dreams.

All good flows your way.

Noisy Voices

If I decide to learn something new today, what if I do it all wrong?
What if I feel inadequate? What if I feel too much pressure? What if
someone negates my efforts?

Here is an amusing technique that helps us see the chaos in our mind. Write an autobiographical play that contains several scenes from your inner dialogue. The only tools you need are a few annoying conflicts and a bunch of noisy voices swimming around in your head. It sounds easy, right?

One problem. It may be difficult to decide *which* noisy voices to feature in each of your scenes. There are so many of them. They are wise, stubborn, positive, awakened, pitiful, hopeful, negative, impatient, encouraging, rude, scared, optimistic, pessimistic, insecure, courageous, strong, happy, adventurous, resistant, appreciative, passive, sensible, rebellious, fearful, excited, angry, hurt, sad, anxious, witty, wild, grateful, persistent, patient, humorous, curious, joyful, ecstatic and flexible.

Did I leave anybody out?

Warning. The voices that we hear inside ourselves can be challenging. Some voices are too quiet, other voices are too loud, some like to interrupt each other, and the most incorrigible ones are those that talk all at once. What a crew!

Here are several scripts from my own life...

Script #1

The Wise Inner Guru: Melody, what's wrong? Why did you stop dreaming? You know that you are happiest when you dream and create. How about resuscitating your inner heart-dreamer today?

The Negative, Pessimistic, Impatient and Resistant Voices: Not now. It takes too much time out of my life to work on new projects. Besides, I'm completely out of ideas. Even if I come up with one, I don't have the energy or attention span to follow it through to the end. Don't worry about it. I have plenty of errands and personal issues that can keep me extremely busy for the rest of my life. Thanks for your idea, but I think I'll wait.

The Wise Inner Guru: Oh, Melody. Don't you know? There is no better time than now. When you follow the magical seeds of a new dream, your life will be filled with a renewed sense of purpose and passion. Come back to your home, Melody. I can sense that you are homesick for yourself. Honor that starry-eyed dreamer of dreams inside your soul. The world desperately needs what you have to offer.

The Awakened Voice: Great pep talk wise one. I sounded pitiful, didn't I? You're right about everything. I may have lost my way for a minute, but I'm back. From now on, I promise to honor the dreamer inside me. Thank you for the extra push.

Script #2

The Wise Inner Guru: Melody, you seem all pent-up. Take a few minutes to write in your journal. It will help shift your mood. Spend quality time with yourself and look within for a while.

The Rebellious and Resistant Voices: I don't feel like writing. Besides, my penmanship is illegible, I don't have anything of value to say, I'm not sure that I'm a good writer, I'm in a crabby mood, and my favorite journal is hiding in the abyss somewhere. I'd rather stay busy doing other things. Thanks for trying. Stop nudging me now. Go away. Bye.

The Wise (and Persistent) Guru: I'm not leaving you, Melody. I'm like a dog to both ankles. I'm the wise one, remember? Just let your feelings flow out of you without any self-judgment and inner censorship. No one needs to be a "real" writer. Writing is simply a tool for releasing pent-up thoughts and feelings and there is never one "right" way.

The Grateful and Humorous Voices: Thank you wise one. When you're right, you're right. It's amazing how much better I feel. I promise. I'll never argue with you again.

Script #3

The Wise Inner Guru: Melody, how about stretching your brain a little more today? Stimulate those neurons. Any new curiosities and interests?

The Resistant, Insecure and Fearful Voices: No. I'm comfortable knowing what I know and doing what I'm doing. I like staying in my comfort zone. There's nothing wrong with that. It's too much trouble anyways. If I decide to learn something new, what if I do it all wrong? What if I feel inadequate? What if I feel too much pressure? What if someone negates all my effort?

The Wise Inner Guru: Do it anyways. For you. Only you. Take a risk. Have more confidence in yourself. There are so many wonderful things to learn in the world and they are all waiting for you. How about your new computer? I know that you've been wanting to learn more about it. What about your cello, keyboard, dulcimer and ukulele? They're waiting for you too. Oh, and what about Keith Urban? He's been waiting patiently for over six months! His instructional DVDs have been sitting in your home just collecting dust. He'd love to teach you how to play guitar better. Challenge yourself. Get those neurons going. I know that you can do it.

The Excited and Curious Voices: You're right. I'm going to make time to play my cello, learn guitar from Keith, explore my new keyboard, register for a photography class, learn to speak a new language, and participate in an inner growth workshop. How's that for starters, wise one? Thanks for reminding me to expand, take risks and stretch my brain.

Script #4

The Wise Inner Guru: Melody, it seems to me that you've spent enough time alone. Go out there in the world. Someone needs your heart-centered attention.

The Resistant Voice: No. I enjoy my own company and I don't want to give it up. I know that I have been in my own world for a while, but I need as much time as possible to be alone.

The Wise Inner Guru: I understand. Over the years, you've given a lot of yourself and you are returning to your own breath now. I hear you. I still think that it would be a positive change for you to be with other people for a while. Just zoom around town for a few hours, stop at different places along the way, and see what happens. Someone would love to have you flutter towards their heart for a while. Please consider the truth of my wisdom.

The Optimistic Voice: You're right, wise one. I love connecting with people, and if I can make a difference in someone's life today, it will make my own heart sing. Thanks for giving me a loving nudge.

✳ **An Experiential Activity:** Using all my examples in "Noisy Voices" as your template, create several autobiographical scripts. After all your juicy topics are chosen, decide on all your noisy voices. Enjoy both the truth and the humor in this exercise. As Shakespeare said in his play, *As You Like It*, "All the world's a stage, and all the men and women in it merely players."

♥ **Life Wisdom:** We have hundreds of thoughts and hundreds of clashing voices. Instead of fighting with them, your noisy voices can become an amusing game of self-witnessing, self-observation, increased consciousness and personal enlightenment.

"Oh yes, there I go again. Quiet down everyone. Breathe. Get centered. What do I *really* want? What do I *really* need? What would be healthy, fun, loving, stimulating, creative, dream-making, satisfying and nurturing?"

Love yourself enough to listen to your wise inner guru.

The Stop Sign Technique

Nothing can stop your dreams for a better present
and a more hopeful future.

♥

"Snap out of it! Just Stop!"

Did he really say that? He sounded so mean. Wow, he sure doesn't match my
expectation of a heart-centered therapist.

Truth alert. Sometimes this blunt approach can work wonders. Don't get
me wrong. I still think that there is room for this therapist to grow in
the compassion department and I still think that there is a less degrading
way to communicate. I also believe that his suggestion contains a ring of
truth.

Do you remember a scene from the movie, *Moonstruck*? Cher was fed up
with her lover, slapped his face, and told him to "snap out of it." And he
did. Although I don't advocate slapping anyone's face, what if we gave
ourselves a "snap out of it" pep talk that was still surrounded with the
energy of unconditional love?

♥ **Life Wisdom:** If you find that you're on an endless merry-go-round
of negative thoughts, just say to yourself, "Hey, my friend. Snap out
of it. Just stop. It's not doing you any good to think like this. It's self-
destructive. Don't put yourself down. You tried your best. You did your
best. Breathe. Love yourself. Shift your heart towards self-compassion."

Who knows? Your "snap out of it" pep talk may be just the right formula for stopping an incessant wheel of negativity.

The Stop Sign Technique: When I'm in the middle of a groaning, mumbling, sighing and moaning episode, I visualize a big red stop sign with my compassionate and loving alter ego on it. She encourages me to stop obsessing and asks me to visualize a better attitude. She also suggests specific activities. She reminds me that at any moment I could sing, play uplifting music, watch a funny movie, walk in nature, write in my journal or reach out to a good friend.

If we aren't overwhelmed by too many stressors, the stop sign technique might end our inner tornado in a New York minute. If we feel overloaded by issues that are deeper and more troubling, the stop sign technique may not be a magic cure. If you've been in a despondent or anxious mood for a while, please consider reaching out to a therapist who will guide, listen and support you with a compassionate heart. There are many kinds of therapy and therapists and your intuition will tell you when you have tapped into the right one. If that person and approach isn't right for your personality, keep looking. Find someone who can help you lean towards living with a positive mindset. When you least expect it, life will shift for the better. You will experience light on your face and hope in your heart. Trust. Every moment is an opportunity for rebirth. Nothing can stop your dreams for a better present and a more hopeful future.

You have what it takes to move forward, no matter what!

Sound Healing

"AHH" will change your life.

Sound healing is a life-changing tool used by in tune *and* out of tune singers. In this technique, there is no such thing as a right or wrong note and there is no such thing as a bad or good singer. Everyone is welcome to release their sound.

When I attended a workshop on sound healing a few years ago, my instructor shared an inspirational story about Helen Keller and her teacher, Anne Sullivan. Although Helen was deaf, Anne decided to sing the open vowel sound of "AHH" to her. As she sang "Ahh," she placed Helen's hand on her heart, and for the first time in her life, Helen could feel the powerful vibration of sound. It was a miraculous teaching moment and it changed Helen's life forever.

✱ **An Experiential Activity:** This touching story was the catalyst that ignited my own curiosity about the healing power of sound, and I have been an avid participant of this technique ever since. Let's duplicate this exercise. Produce an elongated "AHH" on any note, and as you sing, press your hand *firmly* on your heart. Can you feel your vibration on the palm of your hand? If you didn't notice anything remarkable, don't worry. You didn't fail "Sound Healing 101."

Elongate the sound of "AHH" again and push your voice even louder and stronger this time. When you run out of breath, take another one.

"AHH" again. Keep trying. You know what "they" say. "Practice makes perfect."

Success? You experienced the healing power of sound.

Next, combine the joy of sound healing with the magic of the visualization technique. As you close your eyes and sing "AHH," send yourself unconditional love, nurturing, forgiveness and compassion. *Linger. Stay a while. Don't rush it.*

After you fill your own spirit with plenty of love, send your "AHH" of love to everyone in your life. Send it to people you like, and even send it to people you don't like. *Linger. Stay a while. Don't rush it.*

Finally, as you sing "AHH," send your love to the entire planet. *Linger. Stay a while. Don't rush it.*

Give yourself a healing sound bath and let yourself "AHH" away for hours. It is time well-spent. It is inconsequential whether we sing in tune or out of tune. All notes and all people are respected, and everyone is accepted for who they are.

When we use our full vocal power to sing "AHH," it helps us remember that it is our birthright to speak and sing our truth out loud.

This Moment

Take time-out that is only for you and your breath.

♥

Everything begins with baby steps. Even five minutes of meditation helps reduce stress, improves attention span, increases mindfulness and creates calm energy. When we learn to lasso ourselves back to the present moment, each breath becomes our sacred gift. Take time-out that is only for you and your breath. There are many kinds of meditation and there are many ways to integrate it into your life. When the timing is right, consider taking a meditation class. In the meantime, when your blood pressure is too high and your thoughts are pushing you off-balance, do one simple thing for me.

Close your eyes. Inhale slowly. Exhale slowly.

That's all. Do it for two minutes. Notice how it made you feel. Tomorrow, try our breathing exercise for five minutes. Who knows? It may become your favorite antidote for reducing stress.

♥ **Life Wisdom:** "Chakras" refer to the energy centers that move inside us. It is a Sanskrit word for "wheels of spinning energy." I own several chakra singing bowls, and when I ring them, each unique vibration resonates throughout the entire room and helps to expand and heal the different chakras in my body.

Let's use my chakra bowl and its vibrational power as a metaphor. Imagine that one of my chakra bowls symbolizes our mind and all that chatters inside it. Let's fill my empty singing bowl with papers, computers, bills, text messages, internet searches, emails, "breaking news" bulletins, endless thoughts, errands, worries, stressors, keys, glasses, doubts, fears, decisions, plans, relationship conflicts and to-do lists. When I pick up my mallet to ring the bowl again, its sound is lifeless.

Our mind is just like that bowl. If it's uncluttered, we are full of life, zing and energy. If it's cluttered, we feel tired, overstressed and lifeless. Let's stimulate inner and outer vibrancy by uncluttering our mind and inviting more moments of downtime to simply breathe and be. Just for a few minutes, see what it's like to stop rushing around and thinking a thousand thoughts at once. See what it feels like to just "be." Return to the present moment. Here. Now. This. The "I am" of your breath.

Ahh. Peace at last.

Take My Hand

(From the album, "Lullabies of Love" by Cheryl Melody ©)

A worthwhile journey…

Come my friend, take my hand come with me
As we go on our journey
And spread your loving light from above
Surrender to peace and love.

May the light shine upon you like an evening star
May love flow within you everywhere you are
Protect and guide while on your way
As you reach for the light of the day.

May your journey be easy and your heart be light
May you feel peace of mind both day and night
Healing love lives within every precious hour
As your soul blossoms forth like a flower.

Come my friend, let your body heal
Open your heart, breathe the good you can feel
Breathe in joy and gladness and a golden light
Let love protect you day and night.

Come my friend, take my hand come with me
As we go on our journey
And spread your loving light from above
Surrender to peace and love.

- Chapter Three -

A Leap of Faith

*I don't question the wisdom-whispers
that dance in my heart.*

*If I sense that the whisper
came from my highest intuition,
I listen.*

Overpowering the Inner Critic

"Do not go where the path may lead,
go instead where there is no path and leave a trail."

Ralph Waldo Emerson

As we step into the world of never-ending dreams, doubts, fears, hopes and tears, let's reach for the stars…

No matter what.

Imagine this scene. You are looking forward to working on a new project and everything about it feels exciting. You've spent time researching and organizing, your mood is upbeat and confident, and you're ready to begin. Out of nowhere, self-doubt and fear invade your psyche. What just happened? You were fine a minute ago. Who are all these annoying backseat drivers? Where did they come from? How dare they show up and talk you out of this dream? The saddest part is that you begin to think that they are right. Maybe you *are* too young, too old, don't have enough money, aren't smart enough and it's not the right time. You backtrack.

I think I'll do this project next year. For some reason, it's just not in the cards right now.

If you identify with these fluctuating emotions, you are not alone. As I was writing *Heart-Dreamer*, my own backseat drivers marched in to say hello to me.

You're spending way too much time on this project. Why are you working so hard? You're old. You're supposed to be retired. You're not supposed to be acting this way. Do what other people do when they get older. Why can't you be more like them? Shape up. Get with society's program. It's time for the young ones now. Relax. Slow down. What's wrong with you? You're not normal. Do what normal people do.

I'm embarrassed to admit that my ramblings are just a partial glimpse into the window of my mind. Do I allow these doubts and fears stop me from stepping into life, love, creativity and dreams? Not a chance. Don't allow them to stop your momentum either.

Is fear a form of self-sabotage? Are the voices of self-doubt irrational stories that simply take up precious mind space? Why can't our lives be easier? Although I'm not a therapist, I have a theory about the source of our inner tug-of-war. Have you ever been scarred by the impact of someone's words? Unhelpful messages penetrate deep into our soul and often poison our self-confidence.

Do any of these "warnings" sound familiar?

Don't try that. You'll get hurt.

There's no money in that career. You won't like it. Mark my words.

You're not being a good wife (child, husband, parent, grandparent).

A woman's place is in the home.

It's all your fault.

Shame on you. Boys and men don't cry.

Get your head out of the clouds.

What? You got a B? You need to work harder.

I'm disappointed in you.

You're too old (young). Normal people don't do that.

I don't want to hear about that. Just tell me all the good things.

You aren't college material. Set your sights lower.

You are much too sensitive.

Just be quiet.

Even as I write these words, my stomach churns and my heart breaks. Negative words cut through to our core and hold us back from being all that we can be. Positive words encourage us to step into our full potential. They help us rise beyond the scars of life and into an "I can do anything" attitude. I know from first-hand experience that it is possible to override negative messages and transform them into action-oriented affirmations. Look at the "before" and "after" in the following negative and positive statements.

Before: Normal people don't do that.

After: I have the power to define who I am.

Before: Do more. Be more.

After: I am my breath. I am love. I am enough. I am.

Before: Look at those wrinkles (pimples; flaws).

After: I accept myself exactly as I am. I am beautiful.

Before: Dumb down.

After: I stand in my full power.

Before: Don't tell them about your accomplishments. It might make them feel bad.

After: I stand in my light. I am proud of who I am.

Before: Don't do that. You'll get hurt.

After: I live my life with courage and strength.

Words Matter.

♥ **Life Wisdom:** Believe in yourself. Don't listen to those naysayers from your past or present. Change their messages around. Breathe in a healthy dose of stubbornness, determination and resilience. Hold your head high and say, "None of those words were ever true about me. I have what it takes to make a positive impact. Get ready world." Tell yourself different stories and create new visions. Step into the freedom of your beautiful butterfly spirit and take a leap of faith towards your dreams. I believe in you. I want to make sure that when the gong rings and the trumpet resounds, you are ready to step forward into all of life's magic.

Sing a different tune.

What Time is It?

Every decision that I have ever made took a giant leap of faith.

♥

As we walk towards living the dreams in our heart, what can we do to diminish the power of our negative inner critic? Is this the right time to pursue an idea, and if it is, how do we breathe in the courage to take a leap of faith and jump right in? If it isn't the right time, then what?

Look Within: What if your fears reflect a bit of harsh reality? What if you are anxious for a good reason? To gain deeper insight into these questions, reach for all the "healing from inside-out" tools. Write in your journal, visualize, create positive affirmations, meditate, and leave time to listen to what your heart wants to say to you. Meditative "inside-out" approaches discern which thoughts and feelings are irrational and which thoughts and feelings are rooted in a legitimate need for better timing.

Maybe it IS time to rest, renew and regroup...

Caterpillar Time: If you decide that it's not the right time to dive into a project, use that time to daydream. Enjoy the caterpillar stage of promise, patience and potential. Set aside moments for naps, solitude and personal reflection. Read inspirational self-help books, receive heal-ing bodywork, breathe in all the healing sights and sounds from nature, exercise, reach out to a heart-centered therapist, and express your feelings and thoughts by writing them all down in a journal. If you have the urge to socialize with others, register for workshops, join communities of like-minded people, attend plays and concerts, enjoy uplifting friends, and surround yourself with the lightness of children.

A New Perspective: Now that I have convinced you to stay in your comfort zone, I'm going to confuse you by arguing for the other side. What if it *is* the right time for change, growth and productivity? How will you know? What questions can you ask yourself for inner guidance?

Inner processing isn't about over-analyzing ourselves. Inner processing invites self-discovery and self-awareness. Encourage your curious nature to look within. What if you **could** move through and beyond your doubts and fears?

What if the timing IS right? It's just not perfect.

Despite imperfect timing, lack of emotional support, negative self-talk, slim financial resources and unhelpful people, is it time for you to find a way to honor your dreams anyway? Should you interview for a new job? If you get an offer, should you quit the old one? Even if you're afraid to travel, is it time to push yourself and go on an adventure anyway? What should you do about your relationship? Is it time to have a heart-to-heart, go to counseling, take a workshop, or gently let go of each other?

Let's breathe in the positive energy of personal growth and transformation. Become the essence of your butterfly spirit and begin to dream bigger dreams...

Butterfly Time: Suspend disbelief. Everything is possible. Would you like to go back to school, return to work, buy a farm, live by the sea, learn an instrument, start a family, write a book, build a log cabin, become a fishing guide, finish your painting, or compose a new piece of music? Would you prefer to participate in causes for social justice, raise awareness about environmental issues, patent an invention, run for political office, create a parenting support group, volunteer at an animal rescue center, or join a choir? How about finding a way to house and feed the homeless, help needy children, teach your own workshop, start your own company, counsel veterans, become a motivational speaker, join a community theatre, or create a writing group?

Invite possibility and hope into your life.

♥ **Life Wisdom:** *You mean I could DO that? I could patent my OWN invention? Start my OWN company? Teach my OWN workshop? ME? I don't HAVE to stay stuck? I can become THAT empowered?*

YES! This might be a perfectly imperfect time to implement a new vision for your life. Every decision that I have ever made required a giant leap of faith. It took a leap of faith when I chose my first job, changed jobs, created new careers, ended relationships, started new ones, stood up for myself, listened to advice, didn't listen to advice, healed myself, moved on, got married, decided to have children, and wrote this book.

A leap of faith isn't easy. It takes trust in the unknown, an open and willing heart, determination, courage, self-belief and intuitive wisdom.

If you have dreams that won't leave your heart, invite them into your life even more. You don't need to leap into anything right away. Allow your dreams to percolate. Order a cup of gentle patience, a gradual action plan, evolve at your own pace, and trust.

✶ **An Experiential Activity:** Think back on your life. Acknowledge a time when you took a leap of faith and it worked out beautifully. As you remember this special moment, put the palm of your hand on your heart and give yourself a brain and body cue that says, *"Job well done!"* To honor and love yourself more often, repeat this self-affirming exercise as frequently as possible.

For dessert, here is an excerpt from an inspiring poem by author, Dr. Geraldine Schwartz.

"Of My Life"

Be gone you timid heart!
Wonderful
Needs
Another kind
Of strength.

Let the trumpet play courage songs
That I may march
Head high.

Let each muscle in
Newly grown wings
Pull its weight.

That I may gather
Every ounce of fuel
For lift off.

-Journeys of Second Adulthood

The Mystical Magic of the Unknown

Is every outcome in life explainable?

♥

Are you a realist? Do you explain an unexpected outcome from the perspective of coincidence and pure luck? Are you more "ethereal?" Do you believe that life's twists and turns are caused by something more mystical and unexplainable? Because there is no real proof either way, you may have moments in which you vacillate between the two philosophies.

Here are two hypothetical stories. How would you explain them?

You're finally retired, and to expand your interest in writing, you decide to take a poetry class. After all, what do you have to lose? Lo and behold, poems flow through you at a rapid pace and your instructor encourages you to publish them. Miraculously, Oprah discovers your book of poetry on Amazon and she wants to promote you right away. *Change of plans?*

Your parents do whatever it takes to send you to law school. You are grateful for their support, but their financial sacrifice weighs heavily on your spirit. Their high expectations prevent you from being honest with them about one of your passions. You are part of a popular band as the lead singer, and in your heart, you really want to sing for a living. One night you're rehearsing with your band and a prominent agent in the music industry just happens to walk into the room. He is overwhelmed by your talent and wants you to consider an exciting idea right away. *Change of plans?*

Is every shift in life's direction explainable? Is there a mystical energy somewhere in the universe that guides us? Although I wrestle with more open-ended questions than definitive answers, I lean towards the idea of a magical and mysterious energy at play.

♥ **Life Wisdom:** I don't question the wisdom-whispers that dance in my heart. If I sense that the whisper came from my highest intuition, I listen. Wherever the whisper leads, I follow.

- *Even if* I am insecure, fearful and insufficiently knowledgeable, when I hear a whisper that aligns with my core values, I vibrate a resounding *YES!*

- If I have an intuitive feeling that the knock on my door of dreams is a mystical push toward my next steps in life, I say *YES!*

- If I sense that this dream will uplift the human spirit, I say *YES!*

- If I know that it will expand me as a human being, I say *YES!*

- If I feel that my new vision will stimulate and expand my passion and creative energy, I say *YES!*

YES affirms that we are open and willing

to step towards the unknown.

YES is a nod of agreement to the Universe.

YES propels us towards the passion

of our visions and dreams.

Was it Something More?

*Our third eye wisdom understands everything
without knowing anything.*

♥

As you read my autobiographical stories, think about your own life. Was every situation and its outcome a result of pure coincidence, or was it "Something More?"

- I was driving on the highway and my car hit an oil slick. After spinning around for several minutes, the car suddenly stopped and my door opened.

It was a busy highway. Why didn't my car crash into other drivers? Why didn't it catapult over the ravine? Should I interpret my glorious outcome as pure luck, or should I interpret it as "Something More?"

- I wasn't looking for a relationship, but when I met "him," something inside me said "he's the one." I just knew. *How* did I "know?" Where does this intuitive sense come from?

I loved being a mom. I also missed teaching music to children. Suddenly, I thought of an idea that might be a win-win solution…

What if I design a music school geared for babies through age five? My own children could participate. It would be the best of both worlds. I'll develop an early childhood music, movement and imagination curriculum, take the risk, and see how it goes.

First, I invited families from my neighborhood to come to our home and participate in my classes for free. My classes were surprisingly successful, there was even a waiting list, and I needed to rent a space right away. My studio became the exciting birth of a new music school for young children called "The Children's Music Workshop, Inc."

How did this dream come true?

Did I follow the whispers that stirred in my heart? *YES!*

Did I visualize this dream in advance? *YES!*

Did I take a leap of faith? *I sure did, and it was scary!*

Did I follow my intuition every step of the way? *YES!*

Was there a mystical element involved? *It felt like it.*

- I enjoyed being a music teacher and I was sure that it would be my only career. Ironically, the universe seemed to have a different plan. Although I didn't have it on my dream list to become a composer, original songs started whooshing through me wherever I went.

What is this about? Where is it leading? Why am I being pushed to follow something new?

Despite initial resistance, I started to daydream about making an album. As soon as I thought of it, my mind tormented me...

What do I need to do? I don't know anything about that world. How much will it cost? Are my songs good enough? Is my voice good enough?

Exactly ONE day later, the phone rang…

Hi. My name is Matt. Do you need a guitar teacher there?

No, I don't. Sorry, Matt. What else do you do?

I'm a sound engineer. I have a recording studio in my home.

That's incredible. I was just thinking about making my first album.

I'd be happy to help you with that.

Great. Let's set up a meeting together.

The end-result? Matt Boland patiently engineered my first children's album, "Songs that Make the Heart Feel Good." Nine other albums now float around the planet to keep it company.

Did this outcome evolve as a matter of coincidence, or was it guided by "Something More?"

- After I released this album, one of my friends wanted to know when I was going to perform these songs in public. My inner rebel came marching in.

Wasn't it enough just to record an album?

Despite my mild protests, I stayed in bed longer the next morning, and with my eyes closed and my imagination open, I envisioned every detail of "*The Musical Imagination Adventure Concert.*" I didn't have any time to tell people about my new idea, and until that morning, *I* didn't even know that I would become a performing artist. Magically, two people called that day and requested a "Cheryl Melody" concert.

How does a phenomenon like this happen?

- "*Peace Begins with You and Me*" concerts were my way of making a difference in the world. I was packing up after a performance and noticed a note on my guitar case. "Call Bob Silverstein. The two of you have a lot in common and you should combine your talents." I called him right away and our bond was immediate. Without hesitation, he asked me to read his children's story about tolerance, inclusion and peace. As I read the heartwarming dialogue, a constant flow of music and lyrics hummed in my head. *Where are all these songs coming from? I better grab them before they disappear.* As I ran over to my new keyboard, I smiled to myself. I finally understood the reason why I was so compelled to purchase this instrument several weeks before any of this occurred.

As a result of our intense collaboration, I created an album called "World Peace-The Children's Dream." Shortly after, I gave birth to several more albums, a musical peace play and an anti-bullying concert. My many layers of creativity were a result of serendipitous alignment, abundant support, creative inspiration and the guidance from "other worldly elements."

Unexpected? *Yes!* Intense? *Yes!* A surprise? *No!* The mysterious magic of the universe was at play.

- Shortly after the Federal Building was bombed in Oklahoma City, I received a call from Dr. Norma Leslie. She was a heart-centered professor from the University of Oklahoma who wanted to do something that would help heal the grieving community. She invited me to perform a concert of hope, healing and unity, and because I sensed that Dr. Leslie's request was directed by a whisper from the universe,

I agreed to come right away. It was held in an outdoor amphitheater, and as I stepped on the stage, my heart ached with doubt.

After a tragedy of this magnitude, how can my music really help? What can I say that can make a real difference to someone? There is nothing. The darkness is too dark. I doubt that I can lift anyone up towards light and hope at this time.

As I waited for the sound engineer to give me the nod to perform, a beautiful butterfly suddenly flew on my microphone, lingered there, fluttered around my body, and then gently landed on my left shoulder. It felt as if the universe had just sent me a gift earmarked, "Special Delivery." I knew that the butterfly was meant just for me. I also knew that it was sent as a mystical whisper of encouragement. From that moment on, all my doubts disappeared.

As I sang my "One Planet" song with the audience, I heard a strong inner voice. *Don't leave these beautiful people isolated in their grief. Find a way to connect them.*

I asked the audience to step off the bleachers, and much to my own amazement, they did. They sang and cried and hugged and introduced themselves to each other, and in one magical moment of healing and hope, we all became a community of love.

- The idea for this book popped into my life out of nowhere. While I was folding laundry, I suddenly saw **Heart-Dreamer** flash through my mind. The hyphen symbol seemed important. I had a strong feeling that it was there to emphasize the connection between our heart and all our dreams.

My questioning mind struggled...

Why did these two words and its hyphen symbol show up in my mind at all today? After all, I was just innocently folding laundry and minding my own business. What just happened and what am I supposed to do with the information? I think I'll ignore it. Life will be easier that way. I'm sure that it doesn't mean anything. It was probably just a mirage that I made up in my imagination. Wait. No. I WON'T ignore it. This kind of magic has happened to me before. Many times. It must have come through me for a reason. I wonder what it is...

Suddenly my third eye intuition understood everything without knowing anything. In one sacred moment, I realized that I had been graced with a wisdom-whisper, a higher purpose, and a very special invitation that said...

You have always lived the life of a heart-dreamer. It is time to share all that you know about dreams, creativity and hope. You are in your seventies now. Before it is too late, inspire the world with your wisdom.

From that moment on, I made an inner commitment to follow the whispers of my heart and the wisdom of my highest intuition. I made a vow to do whatever it took to manifest a book called *Heart-Dreamer*.

✳ **An Experiential Activity:** Have you ever experienced unexpected situations and magical outcomes in your own life? Think back. Can all your experiences be explained purely from a scientific and logical point of view, or is it possible that something more mystical was happening? Use the template from "Was It Something More." Think about all the times that life gave you delightful and unexpected outcomes. Write your stories down. What do you think now?

Although stories like mine could be

interpreted as pure coincidence,

what if they were propelled by

"Something More?"

As Plain as the Nose on your Face

Can you wiggle your ears?

♥

Writer and theologian, GK Chesterton, delights me with this quote: "Angels can fly because they can take themselves lightly."

✱ An Experiential Activity: Let's use his words to lighten us up today. If I asked you to make a list of all your innate talents, I'm curious. Which talents would you highlight? In brainstorming this list, let's take ourselves as lightly as those angels. Here is a little inspiration to help you remember all your lighter talents.

Do you make people laugh? Are you double-jointed? Can you wiggle your ears? (I can). Raise one eyebrow higher than the other? (My sister can). Can your tongue reach the tip of your nose? Can you make silly faces? Twist your lips in a weird way? (My son can). Make weird sounds? Whistle through your teeth? Can you imitate cartoon voices? Beatbox? Rattle off tongue-twisters? Make Donald Duck quacking sounds? (My husband and I can). Lip buzz? (I'm an expert at it). Imitate bird calls? Play the kazoo? Sing to plants, insects and animals?

Any other unusual talents?

♥ Life Wisdom: Live with a lighter heart. Let's ask our inner child to play with us. Blow bubbles, skip, hum, kazoo, doodle, imagine, daydream, dance freely, smile, belly laugh and giggle. See the world through the eyes of wonder and awe. Even if there are serious issues in your life right now, a magical child of pure delight and unconditional love is somewhere inside you. Give her a playful nudge. She'll be happy that you found each other again.

Think about all your other gifts now. You know. The ones that are led by love and lead to love. Think about everything that you have ever learned by simply living your life. Your rich memoir is your story of inspiration. Your wisdom is your greatest gift. Who can share their life and its lessons as genuinely as you? Who can be an empathic listener more than you? Who can reignite and support someone's dreams better than you? Who can love themselves and love others better than you? Make a conscious choice to spread your love, wisdom and lightness all around our precious planet. Allow all your gifts to shine, and remember to include your duck quacking, eyebrow raising, ear wiggling, weird noises and silly faces.

BE the heart of a child.

Pushing Through the Blues

"I find hope in the darkest of days and focus in the brightest.
I do not judge the universe."

His Holiness the Dalai Lama

A Journal Writing Entry: I am overwhelmed by loss and grief today. So many of my family members and friends passed away around the same time and it just doesn't seem fair. I've heard the saying, "God doesn't give you any more than you can handle," but I'm having difficulty handling these losses gracefully. I know that death is part of life, but when we love someone, it's difficult to accept that we won't see them anymore.

On my good days, I know one truth. Our loved ones are around us forever. Every day, something or someone reminds us of their unique laugh, jokes, stories, voice, sayings, songs, personality, talents and words of wisdom. Despite this truth, I would give anything to have them back in physical form again.

A few months later: The saying, "life is for the living," is true. I need to keep moving forward, and my loved ones would want that for me. Before I go about my day, I'll write in my journal. The topic? The "Serenity Prayer." The words in this prayer remind me of two shining truths and it might help me today if I remembered to live these truths. First, the only person that I can really change is myself. Second, I can't fix every unresolved situation that comes my way. This sounds like an easy and logical way to live, but it isn't. At least for me. As someone who likes to fix conflicts and unresolved situations, I am a work in progress. My dilemma centers on discerning *which* situations need to be surrendered to miracles and which situations *can* be influenced by my wisdom and courage. I am still learning how to maneuver through the subtleties and confusions of life, but with a little more consciousness and a dose of patience, I'll get there eventually.

Before I end my journal writing entry, I need to add one more personal truth. I must admit that it has been a challenging time of regret, sadness, grief and longing. You see, I also have a bad case of the "aging blues." Don't get me wrong. My skipping-through-the-meadow imagination, innocence, lightness and humor are still happily dancing inside my spirit. There is only one problem. If I am still so young and full of life, how in the world did I get to be this old? What happened?

I know what you're thinking. I need to adopt a "new and improved" attitude. I'm just frustrated. Like a toddler, "I want more!" I don't expect to leave our planet today, but just in case it's about to happen, I want to tell the universe that I haven't been able to accomplish everything yet.

Please wait a little longer.

I need more time to expand my brain, absorb and conquer new technology, compose and sing more songs, write more books, learn more instruments, learn how to give and receive more love, heal more deeply, see more places and meet more people. I want time to slow down, and it irritates me that I can't do anything about it. I guess I failed my "Serenity Prayer" class today and it's clear that I need to do more inner work on this topic.

My writing entries have been quite a pity party today. I can just hear my wise inner guru saying, "Okay Melody. It's time to snap out of it. Remember the "stop sign technique?" Remember your positive affirmations? Let's hear them."

She is right. It *IS* time to give myself a major pep talk and I'm going to do it right now.

Get a grip, Melody. You are alive today. You are vibrant and healthy today. Acknowledge your feelings of grief and longing, but also continue to move forward. Honor yourself and honor all the beauty and love that surround you. Stop fretting. Life isn't over. It's just changing. Your story is constantly evolving, and there is so much more ahead.

P.S. My pep talk worked. I still feel moments of sadness, but I am also moving forward. I am ready to reignite a life of glow, glitter, fairy dust, dreams, mystery, magic and miracles, and I am recommitted to a healthy dose of mischief. Watch out world. I'm taking a leap of faith and I'm betting on myself all the way.

Live. This is the time. Now.

Hidden Cues and Clues

*"Listen to the wind. It talks. Listen to the silence. It speaks.
Listen to your heart. It knows."*

Native American Proverb

When I feel a desire to contemplate the deeper questions in life, I turn to my third eye wisdom. Magically, answers to my questions seem to appear out of nowhere. Not only do I listen for the whispers, but I also look around for subtle signs, cues in nature, inspiring stories and loving shouts.

There are cues and clues everywhere.

Did I look at the words on that bumper sticker in front of me? Did they contain just the right message for me today?

What about the words on that billboard over there?

How about that book? Did it inspire me? Did it shift my attitude?

And what about that sweet hummingbird that just flew right in front of my eyes and lingered there for a while? Who was it? Was it a loved one who passed away and wanted to say hello? I know that idea may sound strange, but sometimes I find myself wondering about things like that. What message did it have for me? I think I know. "Remember, Melody. I love you."

While I'm on a roll towards the irrational and completely impossible, the other day I was sitting on my deck and a small insect with beady eyes perched itself next to me. It stayed and stayed and stayed. Its persistence won me over. I said hello, asked how it was doing today, and started to sing and talk to it even more. I asked, "Who are you? What messages do you have for me today?" Every time I spoke to this critter, it would blink its eyes. There seemed to be an understanding and a recognition between us. At least it felt like it. Part of me wondered if it was a loved one who came to visit in another form. I have tried to talk myself out of this experience and my interpretation of it, but my mind keeps going back to it. Although my little encounter may sound bizarre, you never know.

How about that conversation I had with that store clerk today? What if his story contained messages that were meant for my life too?

What about that song I heard the other day? Did its lyrics give me clues to any of my soul-searching questions?

Did I tune into the whispers of my inner voice today? You know. The voice that I often push away and ignore. What was it telling me? Did it tell me where to find my lost keys or glasses? Teach me how to love more deeply? Whisper the seeds of my next dream?

All of life's answers are here.

Look, feel and listen.

Life's Jigsaw Puzzle

Life doesn't always make sense.

♥

My writing process is complicated, satisfying, exhilarating, spiritual, excruciating, fascinating, exhausting, neck stiffening, frustrating, intense, backbreaking, bottom aching, painstaking, self-sacrificing, ankle swelling, delightful, magical and mystical. While experiencing a wide range of physical strain, mental stimulation and emotional highs and lows, I'm simultaneously swept away by the magic of creative flow.

Where did the time go? I started to write at four in the morning, and now it's eleven at night.

The creative process and life itself are like an intricate jigsaw puzzle. As the content of this book unfolded, I was clear about certain pieces and where they belonged, and unclear about the rest. All I knew for sure was that I wanted to inspire my readers. I had faith that the rest of the puzzle would take care of itself.

I love to ride the creative wave and allow the stardust of the unknown light my way. The magic and mystery in *not* knowing every detail in advance absolutely delights my spirit. I have an intuitive sense that my book is flowing along naturally and the feeling of being carried away into "the great mystery" melts away all my concerns.

The only truth that I need to know is that I am giving birth to "Heart-Dreamer" from a place of pure love.

♥ **Life Wisdom:** Life itself can be as complicated as my creative process and its jigsaw puzzle. It doesn't always make sense. There are times when life feels like it's breaking apart into little pieces and we can't find a way to glue all the pieces together. Should we give up and put aside our vision towards a light-filled future? Should we invite a new breath and dance towards courage, light and hope?

I know my choice. What is yours?

Community Wisdom

What is on the other side of your darkness?
Can you take a small and gentle step towards more light?

I asked members from the "Shift of Heart" community…

"Have you ever pushed through a challenging time, taken a leap of faith, and discovered light on the other side of your darkness? When you are feeling down, what helps you get through your days and nights?"

Patricia K: "The most profound opening of my heart to my soul's intentions happened when I sensed that I was supposed to move to Sedona. I kept telling the Universe that I'm not doing anything without "proof," and the synchronicities were astounding! Even though my action was totally out of my normal behavior with family and friends, I was there for nine months. It completely changed my life. It raised my consciousness and energy field, and it also created profound shifts within me. When I told my mom that I was moving to Sedona, she looked at me and asked, "Why?" I said, "I don't know." It was the start of total release from my family's control over my ability to totally be me. It opened my heart and soul to myself, and it opened my heart to all that I was meant to be."

Susan: "A bad work environment and supervisors led to my being fired. My answer? I started my own school, vowed to make it better than the other school, and I did! Professionally, getting fired was the best thing that ever happened to me!"

Mala: "I was 24...I came back from France to Mauritius. I came back expanded...but my relatives did not accept me. They wanted the old me... the "obedient" version...the ultimatum was to leave the house or go back to being "a good Christian." I left the house...which at that time was for a woman in a patriarchal and "religious" society...very painful, but I could not compromise my integrity."

Cyndy: "Life is too short to waste it following or accepting someone else's agenda-especially if that agenda involves breaking your spirit and self-value. If you wake up each day with dread in your heart and tears in your eyes, get off the path you are walking on. Sometimes we need to take an alternative route that is *not* on the map. Sometimes we need to have faith in ourselves and in the universe to forge ahead with no obvious plan. Sometimes we need to explore and discover how to make our *own* map. It probably will look very different than what you expected. It may be difficult, but it will lead you to many unexpected opportunities that you would not have seen if you still lived according to someone else's agenda. Dreams and opportunities are rarely packaged in the way that you expect or picture them."

Jen: "I haven't given up navigating toward the shore even though my arms are tired and my canoe is going in circles."

Jackie: "Despite the darkness and deep hole in my heart, I survive to help keep other family members in the light."

Thia: "I used to be a workaholic, but boy have I changed! I now give myself permission to decide what I want to do, and I make my decisions without shame and guilt. If I can't finish a job in one day, or I might hurt myself in trying, I give myself permission to split up the job or even take a day off! So that I can rest, I give myself permission to be late in making dinner. I look for magical moments in my journey of life, making every moment more important than the result. I know that there is a reason for everything, including being delayed in a traffic jam. I feel that the universe is on my side and that somehow life will come together. I needed to hear my heart clearly and not have the pain speak for it. It took a lot of work to get the pain out of the way. Once that was taken care of, I get messages all the time. Some messages tell me to stop and rest. Other messages tell me to get something done. To hear my truth, I must keep clearing the pain."

Mary-Jane: "Several years ago, my husband was diagnosed with Levy Body Dementia. We decided to face his death straight on. We chose not to pray for healing, but instead to pray for strength and grace. We spent hours weeping together, but somehow it seemed cleansing for us both. We discussed his death and what it might be like for both of us. Being doers by nature, we chose to do things in preparation for his death. We arranged for hospice, and I augmented his care with massages, aromatherapy and music. We chose to have only those visitors with whom he felt comfort. As his life ebbed away in the last week, my girls and I stood constant vigil. We reminded him often of our love for him and our commitment to take care of each other. We gave him permission to leave the earth when he felt ready and to not be afraid. He has been gone four years now, and we still speak of him often and remember his life and death with great love."

Karen: "As an only child, I grew up knowing that I would adopt a child. After having three biological boys and multiple pregnancy losses, I convinced my husband that adoption was the only way we would be able to add a daughter to our family. Most of our family didn't understand why we would want to adopt. They didn't understand why we could not be happy with just our three boys. Our daughter was placed with us at seven months old, and we finalized her adoption on her second birthday. We were our daughter's fifth home by the time she was seven-months-old. At three-years-old, she was diagnosed with sensory processing, mild attachment disorder, anxiety, and mild PTSD. Later, she was diagnosed with ADHD and dyslexia. There were a lot of challenges and it put a strain on our marriage. Now she is twelve-years-old and an amazing young woman and artist. My marriage is still strong, and our family feels complete."

Chris: "The impression that life comes in layers is an incomplete notion really. The idea that times of great joy can sustain us through times of great sadness is true but not linear, leaving the assumption behind that one can somehow store up happiness to get us through times of sadness. In my experience, it does not work that way. It becomes most important to find the love, the joy and the best in life when the world does its best to hide it from you. The effort you make to keep looking will reward you with a semblance of peace and more importantly, balance. When you lose what you love, it becomes an empty space, and it really is your choice whether you allow it to remain unfilled. The love in my life has not brought me full circle-not yet anyway. But I know it will. The smiles do not come easily, but the gift of recognizing reasons to do so is something that in many ways is an offering to myself. Having watched those I love take a downward spiral is enough for me to know not to follow. The grace of God shows me a different way."

Three Words

(From the album, "Listen to the Whispers" by Cheryl Melody ©)

Hope. Love. Peace.

♥

Hope is the feeling to keep inside of you
Love is the answer with our words and with what we do
Peace is the vision we must imagine near
Keep these three words in your heart clear.

Hope, love, peace is the way
Hope, love, peace is the way.

If the world feels too heavy to bear in your soul
And your heart is on empty and you feel far from whole
If you're feeling angry, confused and alone
Remember these three words to come home.

Hope, love, peace is the way

Hope, love, peace is the way.

Chapter Four

Secrets of a Heart-Dreamer

When you believe in your dreams,
walk towards them.
When you believe in yourself,
everything is possible.

A new sense of purpose and fired-up passion
can make you feel alive again.

Creativity Rap

(©Cheryl Melody Baskin)

*"Choose a job you love, and you will never have to work
a day in your life."*

Confucius

✳ An Experiential Activity: Before we officially begin "Secrets of a Heart-Dreamer," let's warm-up. It's time to invite our muse of creativity to play. The messages in this rap say everything that I want to say about creativity, intuition and inner freedom. Chant it with oomph and rhythmic beat. Invent energetic gestures, and add finger snapping, toe tapping, head bopping and knee slapping. For even more fun, invite some of your friends to join you.

The first six lines:

The musical style of the first six lines is called "call and response." One person says the first phrase and the other person echoes. Repeat these first six lines at the end of the rap too.

> Creativity. (Creativity)
> Let yourself go. (Let yourself go)
> Listen to your right brain. (Listen to your right brain)
> Follow the whispers of your dreams. (Follow the whispers of your dreams)
> Third eye intuition. (Third eye intuition)
> Whoosh. (Whoosh).

Don't plan your life the day before it starts

It doesn't leave room for your great big heart

Leave some space for intuition

Because tiny seeds give ideas fruition.

Let creativity gel and flow

Allow this part to grow and grow

If you follow this plan, you won't wear down

And life will never become a frown.

You won't burn out, moan and groan

You'll just know that you've come back home

To the place that is heart, the place that is soul

The place that will make you free and whole.

The Magic of Creativity

*"Be yourself. Not your idea of what you think somebody else's idea of
yourself should be."*

Henry David Thoreau

"Secrets of a Heart-Dreamer" is the deepest part of my essence. In fact, I
feel as if I majored in "Daydreaming 101." I am passionate about reaching
every one of my dreams, and it is my joy to encourage you to honor the
dreams in your heart too.

**I wrote this book for one reason. I wanted to inspire you to dream
even more than you do now.**

I remember a time when I received a confusing comment on my report
card. The teacher wrote, "She daydreams too much." Physicist and Nobel
Prize winner, Albert Einstein, would have taken issue with her comment. This brilliant scientist, who was also a philosopher and musician,
would have spoken up to her and said, "Excuse me, but I beg to differ.
Imagination is more important than knowledge. Knowledge is limited,
whereas imagination embraces the entire world."

My teacher didn't understand how important it was to dream. Day-dreams
were food for my soul and a soothing massage for my heart. They led
me to my life as an author, composer, performing artist, recording artist,
educator and motivational speaker. They also helped me rise beyond the
wounds of bullying and prejudice.

Dreams saved my life. They can save your life too.

Unfasten your seatbelt and lean forward. It's time to enjoy my delicious desserts for dream-making. Take a peek at what's in store…

- Explore my unique techniques for overcoming fear, resistance, self-sabotage and anxiety.

- Channel the wonder and curiosity of your inner toddler.

- Tap into a new wave of creative flow.

- Discover "inside-out" approaches that enhance self-belief.

- Learn how to assess if you are on the right track personally and professionally.

- Even if you are shaking in your boots, unravel my "secret" to greater self-confidence.

- Discover a new perspective for the word, *(drum roll please)*, "EXPERT."

- *(Harp music please).* Explore the healing power of my "Magic Wand of Golden Light" technique.

Discover, create, experiment, expand,
invent and imagine.
Dream bigger dreams.

Calling All Dreamers

*If I have an intuitive feeling that the knock on my door of dreams is a
mystical push toward my next steps in life, I say YES!
If I sense that this dream will uplift the human spirit, I say YES!*

In a heart-centered nutshell, here is everything that I have ever learned about actualizing dreams, self-discovery, creativity, trust, listening to the wisdom-whispers, heart-listening, playfulness, wonder, curiosity, risk-taking, determination, the power of focus and overcoming obstacles.

Sacred Seeds: Even when I was five-years-old, I was a dreamer of big dreams. At seventy-two-years-old, nothing much has changed. I am still a dreamer of big dreams. When I notice a new "heart-whisper" coming through me, I keep my creative idea sacred and private for a while. Before telling anyone else about it, I want my seeds of creativity to sift slowly through me and only me. Your creative seeds are equally delicate. Guard them carefully, and when you have the urge to share your newest dream, discern which person is most supportive and least judgmental. You don't want the wild wind of your dreams taken out of your sails. If you don't receive the right encouragement, don't take it personally. The timing and the person just weren't ripe for "show and tell." Take a deep breath, brush off the vibes, regroup, believe in yourself and go forward.

If you believe in your idea, nothing will stop you.

Daydreaming: Daydreaming is important work. Imagine every detail of your vision as if you are already doing it. Allow the first glimmer of your dream to step onto center stage. Become a clear channel for your creativity and follow the whispers of your inner voice every step of the way.

Trust: If your creative ideas come to an abrupt stop, don't get discouraged. It happens to me too. During these moments, we are hanging out in the space between the two trapeze rings.

When we are in limbo, that's okay. There is an ebb and flow to creativity too. Trust. There is always a new dream humming somewhere under the silence.

Make Your Heart Sing: Let's dream a little. What *could* excite you? What *are* your interests? Can you visualize the *possibility* of feeling joy, curiosity, wonder and passion?

What makes your heart sing? Think about it. Write about it. Let all the songs in your heart be your guide.

The Magic of Creativity: I am always in awe when creative thoughts pop in and say hello out of nowhere. An inner voice suddenly nudges us into a project that didn't exist a second before. Although our new idea may lead to a dead-end, what if it doesn't? What if our idea leads us to amazing places and people? You never know. Don't overthink and over-analyze the pros and cons of going forward with your latest dream.

Let curiosity, intuition, trust and a sense of personal adventure guide your way.

Dreams in Bite-Size Pieces: Before I decided to teach music to young children, I needed more confidence. I sang just one song to two special children. My children. They seemed to love everything about their musical experience. Next, I sang my song to a child in the neighborhood. I observed her reactions, and I observed my own reactions too.

Did she light up? Give me eye contact? Start to bounce and clap? Run the other way? How did it feel inside my soul to sing with this child? What did my heart tell me? What qualifications do I need? Can I leap into this project right away?

I took bite-size baby steps towards living the bigger picture of my new dream. Before I jumped full-force into the ocean of my goals, I dipped my big toe in the water first. I'm glad that I did it that way. I have been a music, movement and imagination teacher for thirty years and am still loving every minute of it. Take your dreams step by step. When you find just the right place and just the right fit for your passion, your heart will sing forever. All dreams begin by taking a leap of faith towards light and joy.

Focus is Power: If you have a dream that is rooted in passion, focus. BE that archer with a bow. Aim for your dream with unwavering intention and singular focus. If we allow ourselves to be distracted by every text, phone call, news bulletin, household chore, errand and social media posting, every minute away from our dream weakens the possibility of it happening. If there are other priorities in your life that are pulling you in a thousand directions, let go and trust. Your dream will find more aligned timing down the road. If you look around and realize that you have more time in your life than you did before, go for it. Revive your vision and become that steady archer with a bow. I have learned late in life that if I really want to live my dreams, I need to focus. Focus is power.

Expertise? Humbug! It may seem puzzling, but despite all my years of teaching and performing, I refuse to call myself an "expert." *Expert* is my unreachable star and never-ending quest. When I teach or perform, I always aim for a high level of expertise, but for some reason, I don't like to be labeled an official "expert." Ironically, this unique philosophy perpetuates on-going passion, endless creative flow and a life of delightful curiosity. If I don't think of myself as an "expert," it frees me from any formal expectation. I'm not sure that I completely understand this dichotomy, but I seem to enjoy learning, growing and creating without the psychological burden of any label that might inhibit my natural flow.

Learn something new every day, but don't worry about your level of expertise. As you are learning, jump right in. You don't need to know everything before you step into the world to do it. Take small steps towards your dreams and offer the best of what you DO know.

Know Yourself: What are your strengths? I am willing to bet that you know more than you think. Make a list. Are you an introvert, extrovert or ambivert? What are the good parts about being you? What makes your personality stand out? How is it unique? Make a list. What are your innate talents? Do you have an uncanny knack for making people laugh? Do you have strong interpersonal skills? Do you prefer solitude? Do people feel safe and loved around you? Are you a good listener? Do you like to inspire others? Are you empathic and heart-centered? Are you a born leader? Do you like to work independently, or do you prefer to work in collaboration with others? Do you prefer structure, planning and organization, or do you enjoy spontaneity, creative chaos and impromptu exploration? Do you like to work with small or large groups?

♥ **Life Wisdom:** The more we honor our strengths, the easier it will be to lead a life of self-confidence, self-esteem, and the actualization of our dreams. Think about your strengths, and then make a list. A long one. Know who you are and value yourself. Pay attention to all your gifts, preferences, strengths and personality and use them as your guide towards the fulfillment of your dreams. Each attribute is a golden key. Step into the magnificence of your talents and don't look back for a second. Take that leap of faith. Step into the world with flair and gusto. Keep going. Persist. What is your next action step? What is the next step after that? Experiment with the specifics of your idea but be flexible with the results. When you least expect it, your plan may shift and take unexpected turns. Go with the flow and enjoy your journey.

Overcoming Obstacles: To overcome challenges, I reach for all the "healing from inside-out" tools. I know that they have the power to shift my state of mind in a blink. I use the stop sign technique. "Stop your negative chatter. You *can* do this! I believe in you!" I straighten out my posture, force a smile, look up at the unlimited expanse of the sky, create a more energetic step to my movements, recite my positive affirmations, and project an empowered and animated speaking voice.

When we create one small shift from inside-out, our confidence soars, opportunities unfold, and dynamic people show up.

Caution and Risk: As you pursue your newest vision, do you like to take risks, or do you prefer to approach life more cautiously? There is nothing "wrong" with either stance. In fact, it is best to approach life with a combination of both caution and risk.

If you would like to explore your newest idea with caution, research specific information in your field of interest, study with focused commitment, and speak with people who work in this profession. Ask questions, take notes, and keep their contact information updated. Most people enjoy taking on the role of mentoring. Be courageous. Ask if you can observe them at work. Your enthusiasm will speak volumes.

If you are an avid risk-taker, dive right into the heart of your dream. Go out there in the world and just begin. Be brave. We're taking a leap of faith, remember? What can happen?

Isn't it worth a little discomfort or embarrassment to get your "dream-engine" going?

Embarrassment? Failure? So, what! Next week you will know how to implement your ideas even better than this week. You are taking courageous steps towards the actualization of your dreams and leaping towards the sweet juice of life.

It doesn't matter if you are cautious, enjoy taking risks or fall somewhere in-between. When you believe in your dreams, fly towards them. When you believe in yourself, everything is possible. A new sense of purpose and fired-up passion will make you feel alive again. Learning is a lifetime process, and your interesting personality and persistent drive will get you through all the initial bumps and learning curves. Step into the "show and tell" of your dreams with confidence. In fact, you have every right to mirror this boldness. Your dreams have been stirring inside you long before you were born.

You can do it. Claim your voice. Claim your rightful space in the world.

Nerve-Busting

"Each note is a need coming through one of us, a passion, a longing-pain. Remember the Lips where the wind-breath originated, and let your note be clear. Don't try to end it. BE your note."

Rumi

♥

It's difficult for me to admit, but before every program, album, book release, workshop and motivational talk, I'm a nervous wreck. I also feel a slight twinge of anxiety before and during most social interactions. In fact, nerves can get the best of me in almost every situation.

My solution? I created inner coping tools and techniques for **NERVE-BUSTING**. If you need help in this area too, here are a few old and new approaches to add to your inner growth toolkit.

A Wake-Up Call: When we are anxious, we forget to breathe. Our breathing becomes too shallow, our stomach begins to churn, we can't think straight, and we don't feel a connection to our body. When we develop these symptoms, it is our built-in alarm system telling us to slow down, ground ourselves and breathe.

A Meditation for Breathing and Grounding: To feel grounded again, sit in a comfortable chair, take off your socks, and massage your feet for a while. When you feel ready, uncross your legs, place both feet solidly on the ground, and sense the energy of the earth supporting you. Now close your eyes, and with your feet still firmly planted on the ground, inhale slowly and pause. Exhale slowly and pause. As you inhale and exhale, feel yourself inside every moment of every breath. As you continue to breathe, notice the space *between* each breath. As you notice each space, consciously relax your body even more. Unclench your jaw and teeth, relax your neck and shoulders, unfurl your eyebrows, and continue to breathe. Repeat this exercise as long and as often as needed.

Movement: If you find that your energy level is low, invite simple activities into your life. Stomp the ground. Dance. Run. Walk. Dig in your garden. Participate in yoga classes. Conduct an imaginary orchestra. Do anything that will uplift your energy and shift your mood.

Mantras: Here are two anti-anxiety mantras. "Slow breath in. Slow breath out." "In between the space of my next breath, my entire body relaxes."

This Moment: Return to the present. Here. Now. This. Release the past and release the future. Return to your breath and return to this very special moment.

Be Gentle with Yourself: Know in your heart that you are whole and beautiful just as you are. You are a child of the universe. You may have had a meltdown, but you have the healing tools and the determination to transcend all your inner challenges.

It's Wise Inner Guru Time: For this experiential activity, see yourself as two people. You are your usual self and you are also your own wise inner guru who listens and guides you when you feel most in need. I often have conversations with her verbally and in my journal. Imagine this scene. You have been feeling confused and stressed lately and your wise inner guru asks you to describe the root of your problem. Although it is difficult for you to put your emotions into adequate words, you try to discern a sense of clarity amid your confusion. After thinking about it a little, you believe that your uneasiness is rooted by many issues rolled into one. You had the honor and the responsibility of taking care of your parents for many years, and because of this experience, you witnessed the aging process. Now that you are getting up there in age yourself, you find yourself worrying about your own fate with future illness, dementia and losing your independence. Your inner guru listens to you patiently and then asks you to describe the good parts of aging. Are there any good things at all?

You say, "Well, my age gives me certain freedom. When I don't want to do something, I have learned how to say no. As a matter of fact, it's easy as pie now. I know who I am, and I know what I want. Let's see. What else? I can eat chocolate cake for breakfast. I can eat whatever I want whenever I want, go to sleep and wake up when I want, release my tendency to "people please," be more honest about my needs, dance in the rain, chase a rainbow, pick a flower and put it in my hair, get a tattoo, watch the butterflies, and make a perfect schedule that fits my unique rhythm, personality and preferences. I'm old. Less rules. I'm free."

As you list the endless benefits of aging, you are surprised by the outcome. Your level of anxiety decreases, and your sense of humor and positive perspective increases. As the saying goes, "laughter is always the best medicine."

Shift your Focus: When toddlers get upset, we distract them. We give them a toy, blow bubbles or take them for a walk. Distraction shifts a child's mood and it can do the same for us too. If you feel stressed, do your best to stop an unhealthy cycle of thinking. Try counting backwards from two thousand and fifty-four. (Good luck). Walk around your home and look for anything with red on it. As soon as you see this object, sing "Row Your Boat." Change the color, change the song, and do this exercise again. Go for a walk, listen to the birds, and imitate every sound that you just heard. Look up at the sky. What pictures do you see forming in the clouds? Positive distraction works at any age.

Positive Affirmations: To make healthy changes in your life, create new power words. "I stay in the present moment." "Something magical is about to happen today."

Visualization: Visualization must feel like an old friend by now. Calm yourself down by going on a mental vacation. Imagine walking on the shore at low tide. Hear the waves? See your feet walking on the white sandy beach? Stay on the beach as long as you need. You deserve it.

Support: There is only one beautiful you and it's up to you to take care of yourself. There are times when we all need a little help. You are a person of courage. A survivor. You have the strength to fight for yourself and the self-esteem to honor your desire to live a quality life. Pat yourself on the back and give yourself a hug for reaching out to a good friend, a likeminded community and a professional counselor for support. Step by step, you are doing the best you can to grow, learn and heal.

Here are more nerve-busting gems that work for me…

Show Up: Despite anxiety, I take a deep breath and keep on going. *I trust uncertainty*. I make a commitment to show up for myself and I make a commitment to show up for others. When there are interpersonal conflicts that need resolution, I visualize a positive outcome, create confident affirmations, and show up to help brainstorm solutions. If I feel insecure about stepping into a new opportunity, I show up anyway.

I tell myself that there is a learning curve to everything. Even if I don't have enough time to practice for a program sufficiently, I still show up. I humbly trust that my intuition, heart, personality, skills and inner tools will get me through with flying colors.

Although I love to perform and speak in front of large audiences, even if there isn't a big crowd, I will still show up. Why? Every person matters. Who knows? Before they heard my inspirational messages of hope and love, someone in the audience may have felt that their life was hopeless. If I can make a difference in one person's life, it's worth showing up.

Let Go: In every aspect of life, let go of the outcome. Visualize your life going well. Do everything that you can to make it go well. Then, let go.

Love, healing, trust and surrender are paths toward inner peace and freedom.

Get Out of your Own Way: It's a tall order but make every effort to get out of your own way. Negative energy blocks the path towards life's positive pulse. Become your own life coach and give yourself pep talks every day.

Eat Your Spiritual Vegetables and Desserts: Always allow extra time in your life to prepare yourself mentally, physically and spiritually. Use your best positive affirmations to help you rise beyond anxiety, doubt and fear. Release your pent-up feelings by writing them all down in a journal. Stay focused on the present moment and return to your breath. Use the "stop sign" technique. Send yourself the "AHH" vibration of love. Change your focus. Find a helpful distraction. Visualize confidence, calm energy and a positive outcome. Picture your situation going well. Know in your heart that you can do it.

You can handle anything.

Good Stress: Despite what you may have heard, stress is not always bad. Good stress occurs when we go beyond our comfort zone, and instead of having a breakdown, we enjoy a shining breakthrough. We conquered our nerves, fear, resistance and insecurity.

It's true. We are simply amazing!

Enough About Me: Although it is vital to honor the full range of our emotions, it is also important to sometimes say, "enough about me." For example, if I admit to my audience that I am nervous about performing in front of them, I will probably mumble and stumble all over myself from that moment on. By emphasizing my insecurity, I just fed it more fuel and created a self-fulfilling prophecy. The more that I say it, the worse it gets. I might as well wear a shiny badge that says, "Beware. This person is a nervous wreck. She has no confidence at all. That's just who she is."

Instead, I do my best to transcend my insecurities. I remember my positive affirmations, visualize a more confident version of myself, breathe deeply, and feel the energy of the earth supporting me. When it's time to present my program, I create a conscious shift and step into the light of my dreams. I know that I will make mistakes, but I also know that I have practiced and prepared for this presentation as much as possible. I give myself no choice but to embrace this moment with positive pizzazz. I change my attitude, get out of my own way, and say to myself, "enough about me." I shift my focus from myself to the beautiful people in front of me.

I know that I am there to inspire. I also know that my highest purpose is to project the essence of love.

♥ **Life Wisdom:** The same "enough about me" philosophy can be applied to our personal lives as well. Remember to say your positive affirmations, visualize the most confident version of yourself, breathe deeply, and feel the energy of the earth supporting you. When it is time to have a relationship with someone other than yourself, do your best to create a conscious shift, change your attitude, get out of your own way, and say to yourself, "enough about me." Shift your focus from yourself to the beautiful person in front of you. Know that your highest purpose is to project the essence of love.

The Magic Wand of Golden Light Technique: *The Magic Wand of Golden Light* is an active visualization that requires the art of pretending. Wherever I go, I always carry a magic wand of golden light. It works *"for real."* To begin my day, I close my eyes, wave my imaginary wand, and allow its light to swirl within me and all around me. After I receive all the positive energy I need, I send my golden light to every corner of the earth. One more secret. I also use the healing power of visualization to shower every person I meet with my magic wand and its light-filled powers. I love thinking that I can be a magic fairy of healing, love and hope. By anointing people with good energy, I am contributing to their day without them even knowing it. I am happy to say that my "magic wand of golden light" technique works. Most of the time. Every so often I meet people who resist light, are consumed with negative energy, and are too lost to receive my healing vibration of love. Hopefully, they will find their way towards a life of possibility, joy, and love soon. If you meet someone who is negative, shower them with golden light anyway. It may work. It may not work. At least you tried. After you have done your best to communicate with them, shower yourself with an extra dose of magic golden light. It can work "for real."

Share Your Truth: We enjoy adult storytelling evenings in our town, and one night I decided to go. I don't know what came over me, but in a moment of temporary insanity, I decided to stand up and share a deeply personal story with the audience. My nerves wrapped around me and I felt vulnerable and raw. My body shook, my heart raced, my palms sweat, and surgery might have been an easier option. As I shared my story, I could feel everyone's love, compassion and empathy. After the event ended, people came over and shared their own stories of vulnerability and strength. Although I had a bad case of nerves, it was worth sharing my raw truth with everyone. If I am open about my life, other people may be inspired to share the truth in their lives too.

♥ **Life Wisdom:** People need to hear from the part of you that is authentic, real, genuine and open. Share your moments of courage and vulnerability. Inspire people. Show up, take a leap of faith, eat your healing vegetables and spiritual desserts, let go of the outcome, get out of your own way, and invite good stress into your life. Share your truth, enjoy the process, and don't worry about becoming an expert. Above all, use my "magic wand of golden light" technique to shower you with supernatural powers of positive energy, intuitive wisdom, healing, light and love.

No matter what, keep walking on your path of love, dreams, miracles and magic.

Inner Preparation

Look within.

Before I begin a creativity activity, I concentrate on giving myself the gift of inner preparation. I find a quiet space, breathe in calm and stillness, let go of my to-do lists and release all negative thoughts.

A heightened sense of gratitude soon enters my open heart…

I got lost in the thousands of thoughts in my mind, but I'm back to the present moment and it feels good. I am ready to honor the gifts that I've been given and share them with the world. I am here to follow my highest purpose, and I am ready to listen to my heart, my greater intuition and my highest wisdom. Thank you for giving me the gift of unlimited creativity. I promise to never take it for granted, to use it for the highest good, and to elevate the vibration in the world towards light, peace, healing and hope.

A Four-Minute Meditation: To inspire a deeper sense of calm and centering, I close my eyes and quietly recite "This Moment." After I say each sentence, I inhale and exhale. Then, I pause in silence. I am *in* the silence and peace of each breath.

This Moment

(©Cheryl Melody Baskin)

In this moment, I am free.

In this moment, I feel the who of me.

In this moment, I clear my busy mind.

In this moment, it's peace I find.

As I continue to recite the words to "This Moment," a sense of peace begins to wash over me. My left and right brain greet each other warmly, and my muse of creativity can't wait to dance with my open spirit.

I am ready.

What does my heart want to say to me today?

How can I be a clear channel

for my creative flow?

Embracing the Fairy Dust

"Doing the work you love is the dizzying path of saying yes to yourself and yes to a brilliant hidden self you do not yet know."

Tama Kieves, *This Time I Dance! Creating the Work You Love*

My time is often divided. My environment isn't always ideal. No matter what, I remain undaunted. I find any imperfect way to manifest my dreams and frustration only makes me more determined. I live by the saying "make lemonade out of lemons," and I am here to encourage you to find a lemonade path towards your dreams too.

My Ideal Writing Environment: Before I sit down to write, I visualize a relaxing environment, abundant emotional support, inner freedom and sweet solitude. In this inner movie, I see myself alone, quiet, uninterrupted and completely focused. My internal and external environments encourage me to flow creatively from inside-out, and I have an empty and open time schedule solely devoted towards actualizing my project. Whether my book is written at home, in the library or in my imagined hide-a-way cottage by the sea, everything aligns itself with my intention to create to my heart's delight. I write as long as my stamina and pleasure dictate. All of life is in synchronization with the gradual birthing of this book. Pinch me. I am so lucky.

My Reality: As the saying goes, "If it sounds too good to be true, it is too good to be true." There were times when I needed to write this book under less than perfect situations. I couldn't find the ideal place and I didn't enjoy absolute quiet. There were stressful situations, places to go and errands to run. Despite less than ideal circumstances, I found an imperfect way to forge ahead anyway.

I am determined to keep my inner flame alive, and it is my joy to inspire you to maintain that same level of determination. No matter what situations arise, always keep that fire in your belly!

Pause Button: If life doesn't seem to be working *with* me, I frown, sigh, grumble, clench my teeth and make an ugly face. Then, I find a way to shift for the better. I center myself by walking, writing, singing or meditating, and once I release my tale of woe, I am ready to revisit my happy place of inspiring people, creative freedom and never-ending dreams.

Hideaway: My car is my perfect hideaway to create new ideas, mull things over, problem solve, talk to myself, compose songs and sing out loud. Because I love to sing in the car, I even drive around with a bumper sticker that says, "Caution. Driver Singing." This slogan has led to many enthusiastic conversations with other singers and it also gives me another way to feel a sense of unity in the world.

I must admit that singing in the car has its drawbacks. I remember a time when I was driving to Vermont to visit my mother. I was so surprised to look up and see a sign that said "Welcome to Maine" instead. I looked on the bright side. My time-consuming mistake gifted me with the opportunity to sing even longer!

Sleep: Although I respect all the helpful warnings about sleep deprivation, I'm not sure when I have ever slept eight hours in a row. Even as a young child, I created plays and stories long into the night. Many years later, nothing has changed. I extend my day and write long after everyone has fallen asleep. Even "worse," if I wake up at three in the morning and can't fall back to sleep right away, I will write again. The middle of the night with its sacred silence and comforting darkness is simply delicious. Besides, a power nap during the day usually revives me again.

♥ **Life Wisdom:** Do whatever it takes to follow your dreams.

Even if your environment lacks perfection, adjust. Follow the path towards your dreams anyway.

Even if your time is divided, be resourceful. Find a way to pursue your dreams anyway.

Even if you don't receive adequate encouragement, move forward anyway. Give *yourself* permission to soar towards the goodness in life.

Listen to the whispers in your heart. Magnificent gifts are waiting to be uncovered and discovered, and when you follow the magic of your fairy dust, miraculous paths will unfold for you. Expand your horizons and dream bigger dreams. Trust. Breathe in determination, resourcefulness, resilience and a positive attitude.

All of creativity is a mysterious experiment and there is no cookie-cutter way to be you. A mystical energy may tap you on the shoulder at any time. Get ready!

Welcoming Your Creative Muse

"Creativity is piercing the mundane to find the marvelous."

Bill Moyers

♥

It's time for my favorite subject. Creativity. In the following exercises, we are the muse that we have been waiting for. If you are wildly creative, these activities are for you. If you are going through a creative dry spell, these activities are for you. They will help uncover a new wave of creative flow and inner freedom, and on top of all that, they are even FUN!

Before we begin, let's talk about the relationship between creativity and toddlers…

A Toddler's Secret: If you believe that you don't have a creative bone in your body, I beg to disagree. You have unlimited creative ability and inner resources, and you have much more time to develop your creative ideas than you think. After all, Grandma Moses started painting when she was seventy-eight-years-old. Before we explore the activities in "Welcoming Your Creative Muse," let's channel the toddler within and ask her to play with us. I love observing toddlers. They spot a piece of paper and immediately crawl over to it with curiosity and awe. *Wow. A piece of paper. What a find!* In fact, they may be too young to know that it's even called "paper." It is simply a wildly fascinating "something." As they touch, shake, crinkle, fold and tear it into tiny little pieces, every part of them is enthralled. Let's invite our inner toddler to help us approach life with that same vibration of freedom, curiosity and awe. Release self-imposed report cards, negative badges, restrictive labels, rigid self-definitions and self-deprecating criticisms. Step into the joy of a toddler's unbridled exploration of life, love, creativity and dreams!

✳ An Experiential Activity:

Here are several activities that are designed to stimulate the right brain. The right brain is imaginative, intuitive, creative, free, uninhibited and filled with never-ending dreams. Although our imaginative activities may seem silly at first, they are here to reignite creativity, lightness and laughter.

One rule: When you decide to try an activity, no thinking allowed. Don't worry about getting these exercises "right, wrong or perfect." Just allow your creative spirit to flow out of you without self-judgment, overthinking and overanalyzing.

Our Mantra: "*How many ways?*"

- Explore how many ways you can say, "*Excuse me, where is the closest bathroom?*" Be dramatic. Say it casually. Say it with intensity. As you invent each new version, use nonverbal gestures too. Emphasize certain words. "Excuse **me,** where is the **closest** bathroom?" "**Excuse** me, where **is** the closest **bathroom?**" Find at least five different ways to project this one sentence. To have even more fun with this exercise, do it with a friend.

- Can you say this sentence with an accent now? Can you use your best Italian accent and ask, "*Excuse me, where is the closest bathroom?"* How about a German, Russian, Indian, Greek or Yiddish accent? Travel around the globe. For extra fun, remember to use dramatic gestures.

- *Gibberish*: Have you ever heard of a nonsense language called "gibberish?" Babies and toddlers speak gibberish fluently. Although gibberish is an invented language with no rules, grammar, spelling, punctuation or sentence structure, it sounds like something amazing anyway. As you continue to ask for directions to the closest bathroom, invent your own version of gibberish. Let this new language simply roll off your tongue. Let go of any inner censorship and remember to add your wild gestures. Although gibberish is spoken verbally, here is what it might look like visually.

Jkalupa ookalamuna, seplamadeena uttah kematulana?

Now it's your turn to speak "gibberish," and *please* feel free to expand the subject! No more bathrooms. Oh, and if you want more laughter in your life, how about finding a friend that might be willing to speak gibberish with you? It's fun, and there are many "serious" benefits too. One more thing. While you are "conversing" together, remember to use your nonverbal gestures too. It's the delicious frosting on your creative upside-down cake. I have found that if you speak gibberish in public, people often think that you're speaking a foreign language, your creative flow opens, tears roll down your face with laughter, and sometimes you understand each other better than usual!

All my "free yourself to be yourself" exercises were designed to bring out your playful, silly, creative and curious inner toddler. Now that you have been introduced to them, here are a few more activities to reignite your muse of creativity...

- How many ways can you clap your hands? And another way? And another way?

- Attention music lovers! This activity is designed for both non-musicians and musicians. You are about to discover the music that has always lived inside you, and guess what? Note reading *isn't* preferred. Without overthinking any part of this exercise, compose an eight-note tune. If more than eight notes come out, let it soar. Allow your melody to evolve from inside-out. Hum, sing, play, kazoo or whistle your new tune, and above all, don't work hard. Your new "symphony" is being created organically and doesn't require any mastering at all. If eight notes feel like too much of a daunting task, reduce your musical rendition to four notes. Whatever happens, it's original and exciting, and there's even more waiting to come out of you another day.

- Enhance your new composition by adding different emotions and textures to it. Reinvent your original tune two different ways. First, make it sound choppy. When you are satisfied with your newest version, play or hum your tune faster. What other changes could you add to your world-famous hit?

- How many ways can you reinvent an old recipe? Without worrying about how it will taste, add at least two new ingredients. Who knows? Your new recipe may taste even better than the older one.

- Is there a new creative work stirring somewhere inside your spirit? Let go of perfection. Simply begin.

- If you are a teacher, is there another way to teach that lesson? And another way?

♥ **Life Wisdom:** Creative one, I hope that I have convinced you that it is your birthright to express yourself from inside-out. In fact, you can ignite quite a revolution with that creative spirit of yours. Long after you have put this book away, keep exploring your creativity. Revisit an abandoned interest and dive into it again. You'll show the naysayers. Once you have gained enough confidence, the sky is the limit. Fame and fortune are calling you, and when it happens, I'll be standing in a long line waiting eagerly to get your autograph. I hope you'll notice me. Although I'm on the older side of life, I'm the one with the mismatched socks, silly hats, expressive clothes, creative earrings, an open heart, a cheering-for-you attitude, and a never-ending twinkle in her eyes.

Here's to unlimited curiosity, creativity, playfulness, imagination and dreams!

Somewhere Inside You

"Inspiration is the greatest gift because it opens your life to many new possibilities. Each day becomes more meaningful, and your life is enhanced when your actions are guided by what inspires you."

Dr. Bernie Siegel, MD

If you lost your dreams along the way, trust that your inner heart-dreamer lives somewhere inside you. She is underneath the errands, taking care of others, the troubles and the good times. Until now, maybe you haven't had much time to think about her.

When you were a child, what were your interests? What did you like to do for fun? Did you like to collect little things? Put them in containers? Bring animals and bugs home? Build projects from kits? Fix things? Participate in sports? Doodle? Act in plays? Learn Morse code? Compose songs? Sew? Knit? Write stories or poems? Take pictures? Play with dolls? Sing? Dance? Read? Climb trees? Draw? Daydream? Ride your bicycle? Paint? Study? Chase butterflies? Look at objects with your microscope? Fish? Swim? Walk in nature? Create scientific experiments? Plant flowers and vegetables? Fly kites? Build forts? Write in your diary? Ride horses? Experiment in the kitchen? Play teacher? Jump rope? Blow bubbles? Hula hoop? Tell jokes?

Can you find any hints from the good parts of your childhood that you could transfer into your life right now? Can you expand a joyful seed from your past and discover an innovative way to create a new hobby, project or career?

♥ **Life Wisdom:** Everyone is born with innate talents and interests. Sadly, not everyone receives the right encouragement for their passionate interests. When you were young, you may have enjoyed singing until one insensitive remark changed everything for you. "Stop singing. Oh, my goodness. You can't sing in tune at all. Just mouth the words so you don't ruin the whole chorus." Unless you enjoyed a high level of self-confidence to get you through this comment, their cruel message and the way in which it was delivered may have ended your desire to sing ever again.

People have often reached out to me and shared their horror stories about the time that they were told to stop singing. It breaks my heart. As a musician and sound healer, this is what I have to say…

*Do it anyways and do it now. It's healing to release our sounds and it's important to allow ourselves to sing in tune **or** out of tune. Despite what may have happened to you in the past, don't be influenced by anyone who makes fun of your voice or tells you to stop singing. It is your birthright to sing and to speak, and no one has the right to stop you. You don't need to be perfect about anything in life, including your singing voice. Sing in your car, sing in the shower, sing the healing vowel sound of "AHH," and even think about joining a choir. A safe and nonjudgmental one. Don't freeze your natural ability to sing and speak your truth. Be free!*

I remember the day when my enthusiasm for art was squashed. The art teacher hovered over my proud artistic work and said, "Cheryl, you can't draw at all. I think you should quit while you're ahead." That was the day that I stopped drawing forever. Until now. Lately I have been having fun with adult coloring books. Who knows? Maybe it will stimulate my inner artist to come out and say hello to me again.

Throughout high school and college, I played the cello. I loved its heart-centered sound and I couldn't get enough of it. Over the years, I had instructors who knew just the right approaches for my personality. They were warm, sensitive, creative, wise, loving, enthusiastic, knowledgeable and supportive. I also had instructors who didn't inspire me. I learned something from everyone. When I became a teacher myself, I knew the values that I wanted to project to my students. My intention was to balance my knowledge with creativity, positive energy and love, and for over thirty years, this has been my path.

It is never too late to develop new interests and it is never too late to step into new dreams. You deserve inner fulfillment as much as anyone and everyone is a heart-dreamer somewhere inside their soul. Open your heart to life's unlimited potential. Are you waiting for the right time? It is now, my friend, now. Don't wait. There is never a perfect time. Life happens. Allow some of that life to happen for you. Breathe in the essence of Don Quixote in *The Man of La Mancha* and dream the impossible dream.

Become an unstoppable heart-dreamer.

Soar!

"Yes" (2)

Yes becomes the canvas
on which life's future
possibilities can be painted.

Yes is honed in the capacity
for awe and wonder.
Yes begins to answer the question,
"What if...?"

Dr. Geraldine Schwartz
Journeys of Second Adulthood

Inner Witnessing

What are your core values?

♥

♥ Life Wisdom: Inner witnessing is a powerful tool that can lead to a sense of deeper self-understanding. As I go about my week, I make time to witness my attitude, values, behavior and personality. To know myself better, I often ask myself introspective self-assessment questions and then listen to my inner voice for the answers. If I sense that I'm not on the right path in some way, I consciously adjust the direction of my inner compass.

Core Values: In-depth inner work takes time *and* reaps huge rewards. To determine if your life is aligned with clarity and purpose, I've provided you with many of the same questions that I ask myself. The first question is the most important one. What are your core values? When we know our core values, we know what we stand for. We define who we are and who we want to become as human beings. What do we believe in? How do we want to live our lives now and in the future? How do we want to project ourselves?

Instead of going through life on automatic pilot, inner witnessing and introspective questioning heighten our ability to know the core and essence of who we are. The following self-assessment questions remind me of the song, "Getting to Know You." Self-questioning and inner witnessing help us know who we are more clearly, and they are also paths towards increased consciousness, love, emotional intelligence and inner growth.

Self-Assessment Questions

✱ An Experiential Activity:

- What are my core values?

- Are all parts of my life aligned with my core values?

- Am I still growing, learning and changing?

- Do I enjoy my life? What can I do to enjoy it even more?

- Do I give myself inner nurturing, respect, compassion, forgiveness and love?

- What can I do to increase my level of self-confidence?

- What is my mission statement?

- What are my many purposes in life?

- How can I become an inspiration to others?

- Is my life in balance? Is there a way to balance it even more?

- Am I having fun? How can I have even more fun?

- Am I willing to take a leap of faith and walk towards my dreams?

- What brings my heart joy?

- How is my sense of humor doing these days? Am I taking myself lightly enough?

- In every situation, am I walking the path of love?

- Do I honor the truth of who I really am?

Revisit this exercise throughout your life. Everyone changes and your answers will be different with each stage and age.

If You Have A Dream

(From the albums, "Celebrate," "Lullabies of Love" and "Listen to the Whispers"
by Cheryl Melody ©)

Look up high in all you do.

If you have a dream, hold onto the dreamer
Fill yourself up with music and light
Reach out to the gifts that give you so much meaning
Trust in your dreams both day and night.

Breathe in who you are, your dreams are not far
And trust in love to guide you
Embrace what you feel you know to be real
Look up high in all you do.

Protect your precious dream, allow it to be seen
Don't let any darkness surround you
Reach out with both wings, let your heart sing
Look up high in all you do.

If you have a dream, hold onto the dreamer
Fill yourself up with music and light
Reach out to the gifts that give you so much meaning
Trust in your dreams both day and night.

Chapter Five

Best Friends Forever

A good friend is a precious gift.

A New Friend

"We ask ourselves, who am I to be brilliant, gorgeous, talented and fabulous? Actually, who are you not to be?"

Marianne Williamson, *A Return to Love*

A gentle note to your heart: As you read "A New Friend," you may feel a twinge of sadness. Hang in there. The antidote and action plan are just around the corner.

A good friendship is a gift. It is a mutual exchange of love, respect, support, compassion and forgiveness. We lift each other up, listen with our hearts, share our lives with honesty, and encourage every dream. We want our friend to empower themselves, and we will do everything possible to make sure that they know that they are cherished and valuable. There is nothing like the closeness of a good friend.

♥ **Life Wisdom:** There is also a friend that we don't treat as well as we should. We are around her more than anyone else, but it can fester into a frustrating, confusing and counterproductive relationship. We often criticize and ignore her, and when someone compliments her, we ask her to find five reasons why it isn't true. If she needs a good cry, we ask her to put on a brave smile, and if she needs to rest, we push her to do more and be more. When she feels the need to speak up and convey her truth, we insist that she tone it down, and when she feels proud for achieving a goal, we ask her to minimize herself. One more thing. Our friend would love more "me time" for self-exploration and personal discovery. She would love to understand more of who she is underneath all the to-do lists, roles and rules. Instead, we encourage her to stuff away this need. We tell her, "Someday. Someday you will have all the time you need to figure out the dreams in your heart. Be patient. You just need to wait a little while longer. It will be your turn soon."

This poor friend. We need to give her support. Can you talk with her? If she knew that you cared, it could save her life. It could save your life too. Why? Because that friend might be the person in the mirror.

Your friend is you.

Wake-Up Call

Let's shake our own hand first.

♥

I wanted my sad lament to be a wake-up call for anyone who might need it right now, including me. If you already know how to be your own best friend, please guide and inspire others. How did you get to this point? Were you brought up that way? Has your self-esteem always been solid? If not, what inner work have you done? What do you say to yourself to become your own champion?

♥ **Life Wisdom:** It is never too late to learn how to appreciate ourselves. Many years ago, I thought "self-love" sounded egocentric, narcissistic and selfish. Now that I am older, I understand its context better. My kind of self-love has nothing to do with narcissism. When a person is a narcissist, they only see the world in terms of themselves. They are vain, self-absorbed, selfish, have delusions of grandeur and flaunt an inflated sense of importance. Although we may display some of these qualities too, there is a big difference. We are always interested in other people and are more than happy to show them our love and support. We recognize the value in everyone.

**The sad part is that we often forget to respect
our own value.**

Each small step towards self-love is an achievement and cause for celebration. Don't laugh, but my action step towards self-love involves writing a letter to myself. Because it works so well, I make it my intention to write one at least once a month. My letter isn't written from a place of ego or narcissism. It is written from a place of quiet self-acknowledgement, respect, love and support. By doing this exercise, we give ourselves the freedom and permission to focus on all our positive qualities. This letter is an opportunity to become our own fairy godmother who waves her magic wand and makes us feel good from inside-out. As you read my letter, begin to think about yours.

It's time to become our best friend forever.

A Love Letter

"There is a candle in your heart ready to be kindled. There is a voice in your soul ready to be filled. You feel it, don't you?"

Rumi

Here is an example of one of my self-affirming letters...

Dearest Melody,

Starting now, I choose *you* to be my best friend. If I only spoke to you with pure love, what would I want you to know? I cherish you. I cherish your wise soul, loving heart, unending dreams, persistence and strength. I also admire your desire to make a positive difference in this world. You've always known your heartfelt mission and purpose. Deep inside your soul, you sensed that you were placed on this earth to encourage a vibration of love, peace, healing and hope. Look at all the love that you have given to your family and friends. Look at all the meaningful projects you have created to help raise the vibration of our planet.

Shine in your light, my dear friend, and stand proudly. Take the gentle time to realize that you have made a difference just by being who you are. Keep your inner flame glowing, dear one, and in the deepest part of your soul, show yourself the love and respect that you deserve. Keep that twinkle in your eyes, passion in your soul, and always honor the heart-dreamer within you.

Your Best Friend Forever,

Melody

Putting a Magnifying Glass on Love

"Life without love is like a tree without blossoms or fruit."

Kahlil Gibran

✻ An Experiential Activity:

Now it's your turn to write a love letter to yourself, and as you do it, leave the insecure and self-critical person far away on another planet. Think about your life...

- How have you survived, moved on and even thrived?

- What is your story of struggles, triumphs, accomplishments and dreams?

- Are there ways in which you could love yourself more than you do now?

- How can you find a way to nurture yourself with greater compassion?

- What are your good traits?

To write your letter, choose a minimum of five amazing qualities, shine them brightly, and allow each word to flow from a soft and compassionate heart. Save your spirit in the same way I saved mine.

Now is the time for you to put a

magnifying glass on love.

Now is the time to become your own best

friend forever.

Words Matter

"A word is dead when it is said some say.
I say it just begins to live that day."

Emily Dickinson

Now that we wrote ourselves a love letter, let's explore the connection between the healing power of words, positive affirmations and life-changing poetry.

Do you express yourself through poetry? If so, thank you for making the world a softer place. If you assume that poetry will "never be your thing," let me tell you about my friend, Judes. Shortly after she attended my "Words Matter" workshop, she created seven powerful affirmations and wove them into an inspiring poem entitled, "*Ode to Me.*" Its beauty and strength nurtured my heart. "Ode to Me" *felt* like a love poem.

Because I am fascinated with words and their healing power, I asked Judes if I could fine-tune her poem. I wanted to design an even stronger statement on behalf of self-love. Because Judes is a deep person who shines with an open spirit, she graciously agreed to my experiment.

Judes and I offer you our permission to use the final version of "Ode to Me" on your own journey towards self-love. We also hope that you will be inspired to write an original poem. Give it a try. Only your best friend forever will see your love poem.

Channel your inner poet.

I know that she is in there somewhere.

The Healing Power of Poetry

"I know nothing in the world that has as much power as a word.
Sometimes I write one, and I look at it, until it begins to shine."

Emily Dickinson

A mini-workshop: I went through "Ode to Me" word by word by word. I would stare at each word until it began to shine. Here is a glimpse into my "words matter" process. The words in *italic* font will be edited in the next version.

"Ode to Me"

Original Version:

1ˢᵗ affirmation: I love you!

2ⁿᵈ affirmation: *I will* always have your back.

3ʳᵈ affirmation: I *will never forsake* you.

4ᵗʰ affirmation: I *will* treat you with honor and respect.

5ᵗʰ affirmation: *You* have my infinite devotion.

6ᵗʰ affirmation: *You* are my best friend.

7ᵗʰ affirmation: I *will* love you unconditionally.

In the second version, I made subtle but important edits. Although this poem is beautiful without my edits, I wanted to experiment. Are there any words in "Ode to Me" that could sparkle even more? Judes and I had one intention together. We wanted to choose each word with heightened consciousness. Each word and the way in which they were phrased needed to reflect a firm commitment towards self-love.

"Ode to Me"

Edits and Reasons:

1st Affirmation: *"I love you"* doesn't need any changes. It's perfect.

2nd Affirmation: *"I will* always have your back." When we say *"will,"* it implies the future. We need to honor ourselves now. Reframe the sentence. **I stand up for you.**

3rd affirmation: "I *will never forsake* you." Delete *will, never* and *forsake.* Shower this sentence with confidence and hope. **I am here for you.**

4th affirmation: "I *will* treat you with honor and respect." Keep this sentence in the present tense. **I respect and honor you.**

5th affirmation: *"You* have my infinite devotion." *"You"* feels impersonal. *"I"* feels intimate. One small change in one small word makes a world of difference. **I am infinitely devoted to you.**

6th affirmation: *"You* are my best friend." Aim for direct intimacy. **I have a best friend in you.**

7th affirmation: "I *will* love you unconditionally." We want love to happen *now*. We want to love ourselves on every good day and on every bad day. **I love you.**

And now for the final version of "Ode to Me." If the words shine and speak to your heart, write this beautiful love poem down and recite it often.

"Ode to Me"

Judes Look Why

I love you!

I stand up for you.

I am here for you.

I respect and honor you.

I am infinitely devoted to you.

I have a best friend in you.

I love you!

Positive, Present and Powerful

Positive power words guide us into the highest version of ourselves.

A Mini-workshop: Because the words that we think, say and write are so important, here is one final "Words Matter" workshop. Notice which of the following sentences vibrate more chi and life energy.

I will be strong is a weak affirmation. Next year, we will have all the strength that we will need to make it through the tough times. How about *now?* We need strength *today.*

- *I stand in my strength* vibrates positive energy and chi. That's more like it. You have the strength to handle anything and everything. *Now.*

I will try to feel more joy soon infers that "maybe you will and maybe you won't" feel more joy. Because "*try*" is the weakest word in the dictionary, joy doesn't feel like it's around the corner.

- *I welcome joy into my life* tells us that you are inviting joy to dance with your spirit and it's here for the asking.

✳ An Experiential Activity: This is an important consciousness-raising activity. First, release self-judgment. Instead, invite curiosity and inner growth. While you are having a conversation with someone, *hear* yourself. Without inhibiting your natural flow of communication, simply witness and observe the negative and positive power of your words. After you are done conversing, ask yourself the following questions…

- Did my words reflect self-confidence?

- Did I put myself down or did I raise myself up?

- Did I find a way to degrade my achievements or did I stand in my light?

- Are my words powerful enough to free me from my old stories?

- Do they reflect the highest version and vision of myself?

- Do they move me beyond old definitions, overused labels and stale beliefs about myself?

- Do they encourage me to enjoy more of who I am?

How did I speak to my friend?

- Did my words give her confidence?

- Did my words demean her, or did they uplift and encourage her?

- Did I applaud her achievements and encourage her to stand in her light?

- Did I help her release old stories, definitions, labels and stale beliefs about herself?

- Did I encourage her to be more of who she really is?

Listen to your highest wisdom for the answers and make any needed adjustments. Be patient with yourself. The more conscious we are, the more we can change. It *is* possible "to teach an old dog new tricks," but it also takes time. To change your life, change your words. Every word that we say and think matters.

♥ **Life Wisdom:** Your inner critic thrives on negative energy and it serves no positive purpose. Make a pact with your judge, jury, backseat drivers and inner critic. Keep them out of the spotlight. If they sneak out occasionally, get your stop sign out. Shoo them away. Make sure that the words that you say and the thoughts that you think are aligned with love. Empower yourself with new beginnings.

You were born with pure love.

Step into that "Ode to Me" love again.

Self-Love isn't Selfish

"It's not what you think that matters. It's what you see."

Henry David Thoreau

♥

A Guided Imagery: You are in the mood for a little adventure. Although there is no chance that you'll get the role in this short documentary, you decide to audition for it anyway. After all, you have nothing to lose. Who Knows? Maybe you have more talent than you think. You take yourself by the hand and say, "Let's go for it."

To your amazement, the casting director tells you that the role is all yours. You can't believe it. You allow yourself to feel good for a few hours, but your inner worrier soon decides to pay you a visit…

They must have made a mistake. This opportunity is just a fluke. I have zero experience. What if they can tell that I've never acted before? What if they get frustrated with the way I interpret my part? And the singing? I can't sing. What should I do? Maybe I should quit this opportunity before I start. To save face, maybe I'll tell them that I'm deathly ill. I need to go home, and I need to go home right now.

And then you hear a kinder voice answer you…

You must have been chosen for a reason, my friend. Even if you're not a "real" singer, don't worry. Just pretend that you can sing. Remember? You can do anything. Give yourself credit for the courage that it took to take this risk.

Most of all, have fun. This is an adventure of a lifetime!

You decide to listen to your kinder voice. The documentary is called "The Gift of Love" and it takes place on a beautiful island. You can't believe how lucky you are to get this part. Your flight, food and lodging are all-expenses paid, the cast is friendly, and guess what? This *is* fun!

Before you rehearse your part with the cast, the director asks you to come up with a unique "spirit name" for your role. She doesn't like the one in the script. You begin to think about it...

Of all the millions of names in the universe, which one reflects the essence of adventure, courage, strength, trust, creativity, inner freedom and never-ending curiosity?

As you study your role, you notice that many of the words reflect your own inner thoughts. She is everything that you have been looking for in the highest version of yourself. Although you've been distant from yourself lately, your character feels familiar and close to your heart.

As you glance down at the script, you smile to yourself...

It feels as if this part was written especially for me. It's bringing me home to my true spirit. Now I understand why I was drawn into this adventure. There is a reason for everything.

It's a beautiful night, the stars are out, the sound of the ocean fills your soul, and you're asked to take your place on the white sandy beach. You've chosen your spirit name, and now it's time to claim your space and give yourself an empowered voice. You can do this.

The cameras are rolling. It's time. Your posture reflects self-confidence and your dream-filled eyes look up at the starlit sky. Like two wings of a beautiful butterfly, you open your arms wide towards life's unlimited expanse…

"TA-DAA! Here I am world! It's Heart-Dreamer. Been waiting for me? I'm ready now! I walk towards the whispers of my heart and the actualization of my dreams. I honor my truth and stand proudly in my light. I am fully awake, aware and alive. Life, here I come!"

It's time to sing your song of love and dreams at the top of your lungs…

Song of a Heart-Dreamer

(© Cheryl Melody Baskin)

This is my own voice and this is my own song
The dreams in my heart are where I belong.

Come dream bigger dreams right along with me
And when you know your gifts, let all the world see.

Share the very best of who you really are
Keep your heart dancing on dreams and wishing stars.

Dance in the rain, fly higher than the sky
Make your dreams possible, let them soar high.

This is my own voice and this my own song
The dreams in my heart are where I belong.

If I do say so myself, I did an amazing job. Even my singing was good. In fact, my performance might even be award-winning. Despite all my insecurities, I knew that I could do it. I just had to believe in myself, take a leap of faith, and make a commitment to step into this dream without hiding or holding back any part of myself. I am so proud.

Before you fly back home, you decide to take a little time to explore this island of natural beauty. While you are packing your suitcase, one of the cast members knocks on your door and hands you a gold embossed document. It's entitled, *"Self-love Isn't Selfish."* She tells you that this document is a reminder to live "The Gift of Love" every minute of your life. She gives you a hug, thanks you for being part of this wonderful project, and goes on her way.

Self-Love Isn't Selfish

✱ An Experiential Activity:

- Offer your inner child consistent doses of unconditional love.

- Give yourself three compliments a day.

- Think of a time that you made it through a challenge, and as you remember this moment, put your hand on your heart. Acknowledge your strength.

- Hug yourself frequently.

- Offer your inner child kindness, forgiveness and respect.

- Give yourself the freedom to enjoy all of life's adventures.

- Listen to all your needs and honor them.

- Offer your inner child sweet tenderness, infinite patience and compassionate understanding.

- Write a love letter to yourself at least once a month.

- Invite moments of solitude for simply breathing and being.

- Create positive words into your life and live them.

- Look in your mirror with eyes of love.

- Remember to leave time to play, create, laugh, imagine and dream.

- Listen to what your heart is telling you.

- Enjoy the small pleasures of life.

- Reward yourself often.

- Visualize your life as you would like it to be and make it happen.

Bonus Points: Write down every step that you've taken towards self-love. Visual documentation is a self-awareness tool that encourages us to witness how much we have grown from inside-out. For each "new and improved" behavior, give yourself small but mighty rewards. Did you remember to nurture yourself today? Did you allow yourself the time and space to breathe? Did you stand up for yourself today? Were you kinder to yourself? More patient? Forgiving? Loving? If so, give yourself a sticker, play the kazoo, do a happy dance, take yourself out for an ice cream, eat chocolate, buy yourself a little something, and take time out that is just for you.

Give yourself the gift of love and live "Song of a Heart-Dreamer" as your self-affirming truth.

Community Wisdom

Be love, shine love, stand for love.

I asked my "Shift of Heart" village of heart-centered people…

"Do you have any tips on how to be our own best friend? When it is difficult to be a friend to yourself, what do you say or do to transcend those feelings? Let's offer each other our wisdom and life experiences."

Autumn: "Instead of using my given name of "Linda," I honor my true spirit name of "Autumn." Creating my spirit name is very deep, life changing, and something I don't really understand. Changing my name has made a huge impact on my life, and it was an action step towards self-love. Even though I accept that friends and family may need to call me "Linda," I am "Autumn" deep within my core. I honor my true musical inner spirit name of "Autumn." I believe that "Autumn" was instrumental in calling forth my inner child. She is the one that wants to be playful and joyful. She wants to dance, play the piano, write poetry and compose music. "Autumn" uplifts my life and makes me feel free to be who I really am. Not everyone needs to change their name to feel free to play, but I did. If I am true to myself, I am free."

Gigi: "Rather than beating up on myself, I treat myself with kindness. I pause, breathe, notice and increase the habits and thoughts that serve others and myself."

Norma: "I remind myself to keep my feet moving, and I tell everyone else to keep their feet moving too. No matter what."

Lorie: "I am my own best friend by saying, "I can do this. I've got this. I am guided and supported at all times!""

Pat: "I remember to take three slow deep breaths while saying the "Serenity Prayer." I am free from my addictions. I'm a real champion and advocate for myself!"

Juanita: "I love my fierce heart and strong spirit."

Ann: "I am in the process of decluttering, and as Feng Shui master Dana Claudat says, "I'm clearing away anything that isn't love.""

Mary-Jane: "I remind myself that each of us is responsible for our own happiness. There is never enough time, money or energy to fill the cups of others. I have to fill my own cup first, and then work on helping others. I also look in the mirror every day and chuckle at the fact that I am no longer young...but I am still strong, smart and healing."

Michelle: "I triumph over four autoimmune diseases every day. I put one foot forward and go. Life is not perfect. I have setbacks. I don't let them derail me. I keep growing and learning."

Joan: "I honor all my ancestors by living a meaningful and compassionate life, and without hiding, flinching or wasting time."

Perla: "I take a deep breath and know that God is protecting me."

Janet: "I live the vibrations of peace and love."

Mala: "Self-love is embodying my full potential in this crazy dimension."

Maggie: "I have a favorite thing that I do when I'm really exasperated. I have named it, "The Whirligig Prayer." I go into the kitchen, (because to me the kitchen is the center of the house and a great producer of good activity). I stand in the middle, look toward the ceiling, and begin to scream, yell or shout at all the things that are bothering me about myself, my family, friends, and all concerns that I might have at that moment. I walk in circles and twirl around!! After I've emptied out all my concerns, I remind God that I know he wants me to be happy, and since he knows me, he also knows that I must feel that everyone that I love is okay. I can't tell you how many times this has worked for me. My center of peace requires that I not worry and obsess, and so I empty myself out in a comical way. It relieves stress and clears the air of all negativity."

Jan: "I remind myself of all the other difficult things that I have faced and survived! Because I am always aware of what I have overcome, my sense of self-confidence never goes away. If I feel overwhelmed by negative emotions, I consciously decide to be optimistic! I love myself exactly as I am."

Karen: "I'm learning to tune down my inner critic and embrace my spirit. Also, because I tend to take care of everyone else first, I consciously do something that is just for me."

Signe: "I have so much in which to be grateful, and when I am attuned to the feeling of thankfulness, it drowns out the sound of my itty-bitty pity parties."

Joan: "Self-love is a joyous heart and a peaceful mind."

Thia: "When life's energy aligns, my heart sings with joy. When I am doing a project, and I work on getting it the way I want, and then it comes out another way and it all fits like magic, my heart sings. When I go for a picnic and the animals come to say hi, my heart sings. When I know that I am walking into something I heard, and I hold my ground with ease, my heart sings. When the universal energy guides me, and it brings me gifts and helps me to be courageous and strong, my heart sings. It's a feeling of validation, joy and amazement. It makes me know that I am always loved and guided."

Librada: "I know who I am," or as it is said in my native Spanish language, "Yo se quien soy."

Janet: "My dad used to say that too, Librada. I think he was telling us to say it in response to people who teased us. He would say, "I know who I am. Do you know who you are?" But it would be for us to say to someone else. I never really said it to anyone, and I still don't get the second part of it, but somehow it made me feel better. I still say "I know who I am" to myself sometimes. It always makes me feel better."

Sharon: "I am a champion because I am moving forward with my new small business despite health challenges. I am putting one foot in front of the other and am determined to achieve positive outcomes."

Cecilia: "I recognize and accept my fears, and then trust in God's love and guidance."

Marsha: "When I make children smile, it helps me remember that love is all there is!"

Ellen: "When I feel happiness, I feel love."

Patricia T: "It isn't selfish to love ourselves, and this type of self-love has nothing to do with narcissism or vanity. Without carving out time to recharge, there is the danger of being trapped in a cycle where the seeds of self-doubt are sown and self-worth languishes. When this occurs, it's draining. It prevents us from being fully present with one another."

Cynthia: "Even though I'm sick right now, I've gotten myself in hand. I tell myself, "I've got this!""

Phyllis: "I remember to live the words to the song, "Climb Every Mountain.""

Shayla: "Love is always the answer."

Lorie: "I feel self-love when I sense alignment in my body, mind and spirit."

Barbara: "Love is about healing myself through forgiveness."

Deb: "I know that Love is IT."

Phyllis: "I am my own best friend. No one else gets me."

Susan: "I remember that peace starts with me first."

Summer: "I say a power mantra to myself that was inspired by the mystic, Julian of Norwich, "All is well, all is well, all is well.""

Gail: "When I am open to an option that I previously rejected, my life shifts and changes in powerful and amazing ways!"

Naomi: "Life's rough moments and hard truths can press you down. Personally, I find talking to my kids, taking a little adventure, or even just going on a hike helps me find happiness and joy in just being alive and well."

Michele: "I like to reconnect with the beauty of nature. I feel at home outside. I love my hands in the soil as I plant, taking walks in the woods, riding my bike as a teenager to a tranquil place with a stream of flowing water, and looking at a winter's sky and the beauty of individual snow-flakes gently covering me. These are all my ways of finding inner peace and shutting out the disharmony in my life. So that you can give to others from a loving place within you, it's healthy to make yourself happy first. So that you can be the best version of YOU, I have learned that it is not selfish to do healing activities for yourself."

Linnie: "I look in the mirror and soften my eyes and heart. Instead of looking at myself in a critical way, I give myself tenderness, forgiveness and love."

Betsy: "I tell myself to be patient with my flaws, and I don't look at them as flaws. I look at them as opportunities to grow and learn about myself."

Kirsi: "I wrote this poem for myself, my daughter, and for anyone with a dream."

Be wild and crazy, my child, because life is short. Jump, dance and play on your drum. Be loud, love and laugh as never before. Cry until tears cannot be found any more, fly high if that is your wish, lay flat on the floor, if you rather. Do whatever makes your heart sing, my child. I promise my love is eternal.

My Dear Child

(From the album, "Lullabies of Love" by Cheryl Melody ©)

Always speak your heart.

♥

If children were raised with the philosophy expressed in "My Dear Child," they would automatically know the formula for being their own best friend.

> My dear child, always speak your heart
> Know you are surrounded with love from the start.
>
> You can become anything you choose to dream
> Flying on every dancing moonbeam.
>
> Ride your life like the winner that you are
> Breathe in life's bounty, reach for the stars.
>
> Choose a life of courage, adventure too
> A life of your truth in all you say and do.
>
> Fill your days with joy, hope, love and fun
> Keep your big heart open to everyone.
>
> Learn from people who are different from you
> Everyone has feelings, no matter who.
>
> Listen to each sound in our world so dear
> Make the time for silence so it's love you can hear.
>
> My dear child, always speak your heart
> Know you are surrounded with love from the start.

- Chapter Six -

I Am Enough

Whatever we decide,
we don't need to be any more than that.

Three Powerful Words

"I exist as I am, that is enough."

Walt Whitman

♥

When I first heard the words, "I am enough," I felt confused. *"I am enough" sounds too laid-back and passive. What happened to strive, achieve, do and become?"*

Now that I am older and wiser, I have a different perspective. I can still dream, strive and achieve, but I can also acknowledge that my sparkling essence is more than enough. I don't have to *do* anything. Just by breathing and being, I am enough.

You are too.

♥ **Life Wisdom:** When we are simply breathing and being, we may think that life is going nowhere fast, but from my experiences as a heart-dreamer, I've learned that the opposite is true. While we are resting, there is always an inner humming of growth, change and dreams.

What if the next step in our personal growth is to love and accept ourselves exactly as we are? What if stillness is the path towards rediscovering our inner heart-dreamer?

"I am enough" gives us inner permission to decide for ourselves whether it is time to become a resting caterpillar or an expansive butterfly. We have learned how to trust in the flowing river of life, and we have also learned how to allow ourselves the freedom to transform at our own pace. We don't need to push the river and we don't need to prove ourselves to anyone. Whatever we decide, we don't need to be any more than that.

"I am enough" invites us to accept ourselves exactly as we are, and self-acceptance is a direct action towards self-love. You are an innocent child of the universe. Your loving essence is enough.

✳ **An Experiential Activity:** Let's experiment. Decide which version of "I am enough" feels better to your spirit today. First, say "I am enough" boldly. Accompany your strong tone of voice with a nonverbal gesture of strength and courage. Repeat this confident version of "I am enough" many times a day. Next, shift your tone to a more compassionate and gentle whisper. When you say, "I am enough," give yourself a warm hug. You are speaking to your innocent inner child. Tell her that she is enough just as she is. She doesn't need to be any more than that.

Just by being and breathing,

you are enough.

The Heart of True Success

"If you could only sense how important you are to the lives of those you meet; how important you can be to people that you never dreamed of. There is something of yourself that you leave at every meeting with another person."

Fred Rogers

♥ **Life Wisdom:** My view of success is based on love. If someone's feelings are hurt, do we have what it takes to apologize? Are we polite? Do we open doors for people? Do we say thank you if someone opens the door for us? Are we willing to drop everything to give someone a helping hand and a listening heart? Are we conscious of the healing power of our words, thoughts, actions and feelings? Do we live with a philosophy of inclusion?

Success isn't about college degrees, money and career choices. Success glitters from within. We may not be a famous artist, writer, athlete, scientist, change-the-world activist or wealthy business entrepreneur, but we are still a stellar example of what it means to be successful.

Whatever we do to help make the world a better place is my version of success.

Success: Several months ago, I had the honor of witnessing a touching moment between Fatima, the postal clerk, and her customer. The customer had just received frightening news about his health. He was scared, and to make matters worse, he didn't have his family around to support him. As he shared his overwhelming fears, she listened to him with an open and loving heart. While he continued to share, she offered him her full attention, empathy, encouragement and understanding. She made a choice to care about the human being in front of her, and in the process, Fatima mirrored the kind of success that really matters in life. The man left the post office feeling seen and heard, and I felt honored to witness a special moment of kindness, unconditional love and human connection. Thank you, Fatima.

Success: Many of us enjoy dynamic conversations with friendly strangers, yet sometimes we end our conversations without knowing their names. This detail may seem like a small and unimportant gesture, but it matters. Even when we are in a hurry, let's take one more second to connect heart-to-heart and name-to-name. Let's invite new opportunities for a deeper human connection.

> *We have the potential to be so much more than just a face and a voice to each other. We are a name, pulse, person and life story waiting to be known.*

Success: I am always curious about other people. Who is this person who happens to work at that job? What is their history? What have they gone through? What are they going through now? Human connection is a priceless gift, and everyone has a rich life story. Let's take an interest in each other. Every person deserves eye contact and the warmth of a smile.

Success shines when we make people feel like they matter just for breathing and being.

Success: Earth angels are everywhere. They come in all colors, shapes, sizes, ages, personalities and religions. If you have had an opportunity to become someone's earth angel, thank you for being a person's light in their time of need.

He fell off the railway platform. Before it was too late, random strangers suddenly showed up and lifted him to safety. She was about to jump off a bridge, and a stranger talked her out of it. The house was on fire, the baby was thrown out a second story window, and a stranger opened his arms and caught him. They lost everything in the hurricane, and a family took them in. They had gifts on layaway, and a stranger paid for them.

♥ ♥ ♥ **My Favorite Life Wisdom**: When people find themselves in a desperate situation, an unexpected earth angel often shows up to save them. Suddenly, differences in skin color, gender, race, religion, ethnicity, education, economic status, sexual preference, style of clothes or the number of tattoos become immaterial. When we're in trouble, the only thing that we feel is deep appreciation for everything our personal earth angel did for us. We can't thank them enough for their outstanding courage and spirit of generosity. In a moment of need, everyone's heart becomes open to unconditional love and beautiful earth angels are only seen through the eyes of gratitude. Every narrowminded judgment evaporates, and a world usually burdened with bullying, bias, prejudice and racial profiling is suddenly uplifted and healed.

Can you feel the amazing possibilities in my visualization of hope, love and unity? What if inclusion, tolerance and acceptance didn't require a crisis for it to happen? What if we could see each other through the heart of love all the time?

The compass for genuine success is defined

by who we are as human beings.

Success is easy. It only requires us to

BE love, SHINE love and STAND for love.

The Joy of Imperfection

"I think perfectionism is based on the obsessive belief that if you run carefully enough, hitting each stepping-stone just right, you won't have to die. The truth is that you will die anyway and that a lot of people who aren't even looking at their feet are going to do a whole lot better than you, and have a lot more fun while they're doing it."

Anne Lamott, *Bird by Bird: Some Instructions on Writing and Life*

♥ **Life Wisdom:** The "perfection syndrome" tends to be a curse, an obstacle, an excuse and a procrastination technique. It *is* important to do our best. It is also important to live without any fear of making mistakes. If I had waited to be a perfect writer and a perfect person with a perfect life, this book and countless other dreams would have been silent.

I admit that it has taken me a while to live my life like this. As a "recovering perfectionist," I understand its emotional burdens first-hand. Under the surface, there can be internal struggles with shame, guilt, feelings of inadequacy, self-criticism, unrealistic expectations and secret fears of failure and success.

If you have a tendency towards perfectionism too, the chase probably began when you were younger, and as you grew older, it evolved into different forms. Let's free ourselves! Let's remember the important core values of joy, freedom, self-discovery, enjoying the process, creativity, passion, trust, fun, curiosity and adventure.

Over the years, I made a conscious choice to let go of perfection. Imperfection is much more interesting anyway. Besides, we have the best excuse of all to be imperfect. We are human. Stand tall in your imperfect magnificence. Let go of perfection, and when you make a mistake, offer yourself compassionate understanding, a big hug, and keep on going.

Whatever makes you happy, soar towards it. Don't allow the stigma of perfection stand in the way of your dreams. Just do your best and let go of the rest.

It is all enough.

Self-Forgiveness

"The more you know yourself, the more you forgive yourself."

Confucius

♥ **Life Wisdom:** When we think less of ourselves than we should, it is usually because we are dwelling on moments of regret, shame and guilt. Serious mistakes are more complicated and confusing than the smaller ones, and they are often much more difficult to push away.

The Importance of Context: Soften your heart. There were probably many dynamics involved during that time. You did your best for who you were then, and you did your best with the circumstances that surrounded you.

No matter what, it is important to offer yourself love and compassion.

What was going on in your life? Who were you? What were your struggles? What didn't you realize? How have you grown and changed? What do you know now? What didn't you know then? What are the broken pieces that you are still trying to understand?

Inner work heightens self-awareness and lends itself to a softening of the heart. If you continually whip yourself, that's not good. You have grown since then, learned since then, and you are trying to do better every day.

Every moment is a new beginning. You are walking a higher road now, and that's what matters. Honor how amazing you are just for wanting to learn, grow and change. Understand your mistakes in context. Forgive yourself.

You are light. You are love.

You are enough.

Over the Rim

"We learn, grow and become compassionate and generous as much through exile as homecoming, as much through loss as gain, as much through giving things away as in receiving what we believe to be our due."

David Whyte

♥ Life Wisdom: The saying, "remember to keep your own glass full," is good advice for all of us. In fact, our glass shouldn't be full. It should spill way over the rim. We never know when our lives may require extra strength, patience and resilience.

Giving During a Crisis: Giving can be heart-opening, expansive, exhausting, exhilarating, disappointing, depleting and gratifying. When you are faced with a crisis that requires a greater extension of yourself, call upon every "healing from inside-out" tool available. In-between the space of your intense moments, allow yourself the time to breathe, cry, meditate, look up at the sky, create positive affirmations and write in your journal.

Everyday Giving: Everyday giving requires a different kind of philosophy. Unconditional giving has no expectations, but ego-based giving keeps track. "He did this. I did that." Ego-based giving breeds anger and resentment.

True giving is from the heart and to the heart. It is done quietly.
YOU know what you did and that's all that matters. Give to give,
and then let go.

Receiving: There are many days when it feels easy to give our love, time and energy. There are also days when our well of giving feels completely dry. If you have no more energy to give, it is a cue to honor your *own* needs now. It is time to allow others to give to you.

Rabbi Natan Segal wrote a beautiful song that conveys the ebb and flow of giving: "From you, I receive. To you, I give. Together we share, and from this we live."

You have given enough.

You have done enough. You are enough.

It is time for you to receive.

Life is Change

What if I stay where I am? What if I don't?

♥

Early Morning Journal Writing Entry: Yesterday, I made a great plan for today. I imagined driving to the ocean and arriving in time for low tide. I could see myself walking for endless miles, listening to the waves, daydreaming, writing in my journal and reenergizing. I couldn't wait.

One problem. As the Greek philosopher, Heraclitus of Ephesus said, "The only thing that is constant is change." He was right. Sleep eluded me last night and I just don't have the energy to drive that far. Although the reality of today feels very different from yesterday's vision, one intention remains constant. I would still like to carve out open-ended time that is devoted to self-nurturing and self-care. What else can I do and where else can I walk, daydream, write and relax?

I know. What if I stay right here? I can walk on one of the trails close to my home, sway peacefully in the colorful hammock, observe my precious birds as they fly to the feeders, look up at the endless sky, write in my journal and read an uplifting book. Oh, and here's a concept. I can choose to do nothing at all. Instead of "doing," I can use my time to notice each of my moments here on earth.

Midafternoon Journal Writing Entry: It turns out that life *is* perfect right here. Every sight and smell surrounding me is healing to my spirit and it continues to be a glorious day. I'm relaxing, daydreaming, writing in my journal, watching the birds and butterflies, and even composing a new song…

I Am Enough

(© Cheryl Melody Baskin)

My breath is all I am
Peace is all I am
Love is all I am
This moment is all I am.

All I am is enough for me
I don't even have to try
All I am is enough for me
I can let in all the joy or cry.

I tried to be perfect, but I know I'm not
I can't even play that game
I know if I accept myself as I am
I'll feel less self-doubt and less self-blame.

I need to hold my head up high
Admit I am proud.
There's nothing else that I need to do
But say these three words nice and loud

I Am Enough.

Evening Journal Writing Entry: I made the right decision. It was an effortless day of joy and balance. In the end, alone time for simply being and dreaming is important in and of itself. It feels delicious just to embrace the open spaciousness for solitude and the sacredness of "me time." The choice that I made to remain home reminds me that peace can unfold anywhere.

My home and my breath

were more than enough.

The Happy List

"Life is really simple, but we insist on making it complicated."

Confucius

I keep an on-going list of all the warm fuzzies that give me happiness. It's amazing how many little things bring light to my spirit. When I'm feeling out of sorts, I reach for my happy list, adopt a new attitude, and voila. I'm back to a place of joy again.

My Happy List

- Delight in as many butterflies, hummingbirds, rainbows, sunsets and sunrises as possible.
- Buy fresh flowers. Especially gerberas and sunflowers.
- Sit still and watch the birds at the feeder. Listen to their songs.
- Take myself out on a date. Enjoy simple activities that are just for me.
- Swing in my hammock. Fly my kite. Blow bubbles.
- Have fun. Bring out my lighter personality. Let it shine.
- Take healing walks in nature. Look up at the sky.
- Listen to life's symphony of sounds.
- Mentor, inspire and make a positive difference in someone's life.
- Walk the beach at low tide.

- Fall asleep to the sounds of the ocean.
- Read an inspirational book.
- Paths towards joy: Sing, create, compose, write, perform and teach.
- Surround my spirit with the lightness of children.
- Offer people my gift of deep listening and empathy.
- Go on fun dates with my husband.
- Dance.
- Spend quality time with family members and good friends.
- Take delight in my cuter-than-ever grandchildren.
- Connect with my loving "Shift of Heart" community.
- Welcome positive and vibrant people into my life.
- See live plays and concerts as often as possible.
- Stand tall for peace, justice and respect for differences.
- Send thoughts of healing and light to people in need.
- Laugh a lot. It's medicine for my soul.
- Design dreams and projects that make my heart sing.
- Listen to specific music that touches my heart.
- Play my chakra singing bowls often. Send their healing vibrations to those in need.
- Stay fully present to all of life's magical moments.
- Daydream.
- Nap.
- Delight in the sacredness of the middle of the night.
- Take pictures and look at them often.
- Go on more helicopter rides.

What are your favorite moments? What touches your heart and uplifts your spirit? How about a friendly competition? Can you make your happy list longer than mine? To help stimulate an endless list of ideas, visualize just a few of these short scenes. For example, the first "inner movie" on the list is a sunset. Close your eyes. Step into this scene and see yourself there. As you watch the changing colors of the sunset, where are you? How does this scene make you feel? Linger there for a while. When you feel ready, choose another scene from my list. Do any of the short inner photos bring a soft smile to your face and a feeling of joy to your heart? If so, this is the beginning of your happy list.

Your Happy List: An Experiential Smorgasbord of Ideas

- A beautiful sunset.
- A delicate flower.
- A special hug.
- A beautiful child.
- The songs of birds.
- An exciting conversation.
- The aroma of coffee in the kitchen.
- The taste of yummy hot chocolate.
- A favorite dessert.
- A sweet dog.
- A furry cat.
- Those adorable goats.
- A new painting.
- An amazing tree.
- Sweet hummingbirds.
- A loving memory.
- A special song.
- Someone's hearty laugh.

- A good book.
- A baby's giggle.
- Lunch with a dear friend.
- A roaring sea.
- A gentle wind.
- A cozy fireplace.
- The first snowflakes of the season.
- The comfort of the steady rain.
- The sound of a river.
- An unexpected rainbow.

As you can see, your "happy" is defined by all the little things in life. Each little joy is food for the soul and is more than enough to make us smile. With an affirmative nod, we have the inner power to shift our attention to all the warm fuzzies in life. When our spirit is light, our soul is at peace.

"The art of being happy lies in the power of extracting happiness from common things."

Henry Ward Beecher

Community Wisdom

"Believing that you are enough is what gives you the courage to be authentic, vulnerable and imperfect."

Brené Brown, PhD, LMSW

I asked the "Shift of Heart" community…

"What is your personal experience with the words, "I am enough?" Please share your honest wisdom…

Debi: "I am gentle with myself, and I feel all my feelings. I don't have to hide them like I did as a child. Whether my tears are from sadness or joy, I accept them. I know why my tears are there, and I honor both my strength and my sensitivity. I love who I am. I am enough as Debi and I feel so free."

Marty: "I look and act different than most people. They make fun of me, but I've been brought up with a lot of love. I have special needs, but I feel like I have a good life and there's nothing wrong with me. I am beautiful Marty, and that's enough!"

Patrice: "I don't let pain and mobility issues hold me back. I've learned many lessons in my sixty-five years on this planet. I know my limitations, and I continue to build resiliency and to celebrate simple kindnesses. These qualities bring me joy and happiness."

Marilyn: "If you're skinny, you're on drugs. If you're fat, you need to lose weight. If you're dressed up, you're conceited. If you're dressed down, you've let yourself go. If you speak your mind, you're rude. If you don't say anything, you're snobbish. If you are sociable, you're a party animal. If you stay to yourself, you're detached. You can't do anything without being criticized. We live in a society where people can't survive if they're not judging the next person. Get to know people before judging. Let's build each other up. We are all doing the best we can in the same game called life. Love me or hate me, you will never change me. I am enough exactly as I am!" (author unknown)

Judes: "Family is everything to me. It is what I had wanted forever. I don't want any more than this right now. If I wanted it, I would do it. I chose to be a stay-at-home mom because this is what I have always wanted to do, and I have never felt like I settled. It hasn't been easy and it's a hard job, but I don't regret it or want to change it. My loved ones are everything to me. My biggest struggle is in feeling comfortable with this, and in giving myself permission to just be where I am. There are so many expectations in society to achieve a goal all the time, and right now my goal is to love my family and to make sure that I am exercising every day. I want to be okay with that regardless of what anybody else thinks. I just want to be present in the now, slow down and not worry about the future. Simple, but that is all I want right now."

Laurel: "I try not to criticize myself or anyone else. Mistakes or no mistakes, I am enough. I'm just a human being doing the best I can."

Patricia T: "I am enough" means self-acceptance, faults and all. Faults aren't faults. They are just part of being human."

Carmen: "I enjoy being a mom, but I also need to express other parts of myself as well. I want to get the "best mother of the year" award. I also want to pursue my professional dreams and goals. It isn't easy to balance both worlds, but for my own spiritual wellness, I need to honor all parts of myself. I belong to myself, to my family and to the world. I have many purposes in my life. I am a wife and a mother. I am also a person with dreams. I used to think that there was something wrong with me. Why couldn't I just be satisfied staying home and being a mom? I was plagued with a big inner *should*. I *should* be satisfied. I *shouldn't* satisfy other parts of my soul. I *should* be just like that other woman. To be honest, I am still trying to make peace with myself about the whole thing. Other people may judge my choices, but I can't let it bother me. I refuse to give myself guilt and shame for being who I am anymore. As they say, "different strokes for different folks." I am learning to accept all the beautiful dimensions and expressions of myself. I am enough as me, and I am proud of who I am."

Mindy: "I know that this may sound weird, but I never really wanted to have any children of my own. The hardest thing about this decision was that society doesn't make that choice okay. There is so much shame to it. I had to make it okay with *myself*. I know that I am enough without children. I wouldn't have been as happy as I am now. For me, that's what "being enough" means. Self-acceptance."

Alice: "My child is biracial. Even though I worry about him in this world of prejudice, I'm raising him to believe in himself and to know that he's awesome, smart, loving, loved and beautiful. I hope he will always know that he is enough as he is. He is a child of God and is the reflection of love itself."

Julie: "Early in my younger child's life, she told us in a million different ways that "she" was really a "he." She (he) just *knew*, and other than her anatomy, nothing about the way "she" behaves seems as if "she" is a girl. We love him, and we want him to have a life filled with acceptance and love. He is smart, fun, talented, loving and wonderful, and I want to make sure that he always feels good about being who he is. So far so good."

Carol: "Even though I was not able to have my own children, I made a great life that included children anyways. I taught grade school, and I adopted a beautiful child. It's been the best of all worlds. I used to feel angry and depressed that I couldn't bear my own children. Not anymore. I let go of my sadness and reached a point of self-acceptance. There is a higher reason for everything."

Diane: "I am gay, married for six years, and we have a beautiful child together. We're about to have another one. I ignored other people's judgments about my life a long time ago. I can't be anyone else but me. I am enough, and love is love is love."

Return

(From the album, "Voice of the Angels-A Healing Journey" ©)

"You are loved just for being who you are, just for existing. You don't have to do anything to earn it. Your shortcomings, your lack of self-esteem, physical perfection, or social and economic success-none of it matters. No one can take this love away from you, and it will always be here."

Ram Dass

Home, home, return to your home
Home, home, come back to your home.

Reach out to the light
Return to the light.

Come back to your soul
It will always be right.

You are loved for who you really are
And you are as pure as that shining star
As that shining star...

Home, home, return to your home
Home, home, come back to your home.

Come back to the love that lives in your heart
Come back to the love that was there from the start.

You are loved for who you really are
And you are as pure as that shining star
As that shining star...

Home, home, return to your home
Home, home, come back to your home.

- Chapter Seven -

Ebb and Flow

*Breath by breath, you have the inner power
to climb out of the rabbit hole
and step into a life of light, love and joy!*

Perfect Peace

Life is singing songs of renewed promise, hope and love.

♥

A Journal Writing Entry: Everything about today feels peaceful and positive. People are smiling and kind to each other, everyone's heart is open, and life feels magical. Life is singing its songs of renewed promise and I'm delighted to be part of its healing vibration. Peace simply danced into my life for no reason at all. I love it.

I wonder why I am noticing it so much today. After all, I didn't participate in a major workshop, read an inspirational book, come out of an enlightened therapy session, or even meditate. I still have problems and the world is still in chaos. Why am I seeing everything through rose-colored glasses?

There I go. Questioning the good things. Just let it happen, Melody.

I love it when life sparkles. Serenity. I will take it. Today is an unexpected gift of perfect peace.

I love days like this.

Chaos in Paradise

There is nothing like an emergency to shake things up.

♥

Preface: *The story that you are about to read is true. To communicate this crisis accurately, I had to look back into my mind and heart and piece all my inner thoughts and feelings together. I wrote about this event in journal writing style and as if it were happening in real time. I also included approximate dates and times. There were many days when life changed every three minutes and each day was a striking example of living life with ebb and flow.*

This is a day by day and minute by minute account of what we went through. It involved my husband, myself, and our son, daughter-in-law, and our two young grandchildren. Every time I review this section, it's difficult. On the other hand, writing about it helps me heal.

Thank you for going on this journey with me. There are many lessons in this story about strength, fear, earth angels, paradise, chaos, love, doubt, near death, life, faith, surrender, denial, ebb, flow, courage and gratefulness. The lessons are here to help us know that we can get through anything.

So, here it is. "Chaos in Paradise." And it was.

My Vacation in Hawaii

January 9: Hawaii, here we come! The home that we rented is perfect for our family of six, the plans are flawless, and I can't wait to get there.

The First Eight Days of Ebb and Flow

January 11: After fourteen hours of travel and an overnight stay in California, we made it. We enjoyed a delicious family dinner, blew bubbles, sang children's songs, and read our grandchildren bedtime stories. Life is full of joy.

January 12: What fun! While the baby was napping and our son and daughter-in-law were regrouping, my granddaughter and I played "beautician." After she was done putting bobby pins, bows, headbands and barrettes in my hair, she thought I looked stunning and we were ready for more activities. My husband and I danced with streamers to the beautiful butterfly song, pretended that we were sick and she was the doctor, played with her dolls, threw a ball back and forth, read children's books, flew kites, blew bubbles, and ran around from one end of the yard to the other. After lunch, we held and rocked our sweet grandbaby, walked to the beach as a family, snorkeled with the fish, and then walked back to the house to rest. Late in the afternoon, we ate at a great restaurant and were also delighted to see an incredibly beautiful Hawaiian sunset. It was a great end to a great day, and as tired as I am, I can't wait for more.

January 13: Our granddaughter has a fever and is becoming sicker by the minute.

January 14: **ALERT! BALLISTIC MISSILE THREAT INBOUND TO HAWAII. SEEK IMMEDIATE SHELTER. THIS IS NOT A DRILL.**

Is this real? Is it a false alarm? There is no information anywhere about what to do and where to go. My son is busy sealing up the windows, Barry went outside to see if he could find someone who knew more information, and the rest of us are huddled in the hallway outside the bathroom. My daughter-in-law is doing a stellar job keeping my grandchildren calm and nurtured, and as for me? I'm scared and no help to anyone.

Initially, I was in a state of denial. *This can't be happening. It isn't true. It must be a false alarm.* Then, I was terrified. *We're all going to die.* After twenty minutes of being terrified, I shifted to a feeling of calm resignation and surrender. *I guess this is it. I need to let go. It's over.*

Thirty-eight minutes later: **ALERT! THERE IS NO MISSILE THREAT OR DANGER TO THE STATE OF HAWAII. REPEAT. FALSE ALARM.**

In Retrospect: *Despite our unexpected trauma today, it's time to move on and celebrate new moments of rebirth and gratitude. Let's make the best of our time together and appreciate each other even more than we did before.*

January 15: She feels much better today. There she goes. Playful and talkative again. Welcome back, four-year-old.

January 16: Here we go again. We bought six tickets for a whale watch and it looks like only four of us are going. The baby's sick now.

January 17: Wow, that was quick. She's happy and smiling, her fever is gone, and she's back to her sweet little charming self again. Let's see.

What can we do today? Anyone want to learn the Hula?

In Retrospect: *Despite all the dramatic ups and downs, we bonded with our family, enjoyed amazing sights, went to the beach, "learned" the hula, stayed in a beautiful house overlooking the ocean, snorkeled with the fish, laughed and played with our little ones, and enjoyed warm adult conversations. Through thick and thin, it was a wonderful week.*

The Next Seven Days of Ebb and Flow

January 19: It's always difficult to say goodbye, but today's the day. Until our next "ebb and flow" vacation, we'll see you on Facetime dear ones.

3 p.m. Barry and I checked into a new lodging and it's heaven on earth here. Comfortable bed, nicely furnished, clean, perfect size, peace, quiet, Pacific Ocean, beautiful flowers, and rainbows popping up everywhere. The epitome of paradise.

7 p.m. We're all unpacked, ordered tickets to see a concert, bought groceries, put everything in its place, and Barry made an award-winning fruit salad.

January 21: He has convulsive chills and feels an intense pressure in his chest. I handed him 325 milligrams of aspirin and we're driving straight to the nearest hospital. There's no time to lose.

8:00 a.m. Good hospital and doctor. We're waiting for the test results.

8:45 a.m. I just heard my worst fear. "Your husband is in the middle of a heart attack." As if this isn't enough trauma to bear, there is more bad news. Their hospital is too small to deal with serious medical issues and they need to airlift him to Honolulu.

We're both in shock. He's staring at me and I'm staring at him. We are speechless and scared. What should we do? How should we handle this? He is trying his best to come up with a logical plan. He thinks that I should drive back to our condo, pack us up, return the rental car, and then catch a flight to Honolulu later in the afternoon. As for me, I have absolutely no desire to leave his side for even a minute. If we get separated, will we ever see each other again? After all the years that we've been together, is this how it will end?

9:20 a.m. I don't know what to do. Maybe he has a point. Maybe it's hard enough for him to deal with his own feelings and he thinks that my emotions will make him feel even more nervous. Maybe it gives him a sense of peace to know that I will be handling all the chaos here. The condo, packing us up, returning the rental car, all of it. I'll catch up with him later. I can't think straight and it's impossible for me to know the right thing to do.

9:30 a.m. My GPS just stopped working. No matter what, I will still find the condo. I am stepping into my strength and holding a vision of giving him a sweet kiss by the end of the day. While I'm at it, I'll also wave my magic wand and manifest a few earth angels. I sure could use their help today.

11:30 a.m. I did it. I threw our clothes in the suitcases and found two people to help me bring everything to the car. Lanie and Andrea not only carried my suitcases and lifted them into the trunk, they also offered me their compassion. We are standing in a circle together. Hugging and crying and praying. Three strangers. Heart-to-heart and connected. Thank you earth angels. Thank you for showering me with kindness and for giving me faith in the absolute goodness of humankind.

12:30 p.m. I'm on my way to the airport. My GPS decided to stop working again, I'm running out of gas, and my faith is shaken to the core.

Will I even make it to Honolulu? My driving is erratic. What if I get into an accident? Wouldn't it be ironic if I'm the one who dies, and he is the one who lives? Life can be crazy that way. I'm not sure about anything anymore.

1:05 p.m. My son called to tell me that they booked my flight to Honolulu, secured ground transportation and made my hotel reservation. His words moved me to tears. It looks like a few more earth angels flew in to save me.

1:10 p.m. The doctor called. "Your husband had a successful operation. A stent. He did fine."

An operation? A stent? What did the doctor mean when he said, "he did fine?" Could he have died today?

1:35 p.m. The stress I'm feeling is unbearable. While fighting with my mind to try and visualize a positive outcome, my teeth are chattering, I'm crying, screaming, sweating, shivering, talking out loud, praying, determined, weak, strong, vulnerable and scared. To top it off, I just took a wrong turn. I am driving up a steep hill, there is no place to turn around, and I don't have any idea where I'm going. Does this car have enough pep to even make it up this hill?

1:50 p.m. That was lucky. It led me to the right highway after all.

Okay, breathe. Think. What's next? Once I get to the airport, I have a lot of to-dos on my plate. I need to return my rental car, unload three heavy suitcases and two backpacks, lug them on and off the airport shuttle, check into the departure terminal and then get my boarding pass. My flight leaves at 3:00 p.m. If I don't make it, then what?

2:15 p.m. Lisa went way beyond the call of duty. She checked in my rental car, listened patiently to my story, and without any hesitation, drove me directly to the departure terminal. When I began my day, I asked the universe to send me a few earth angels to make my life a little easier. Lisa is my fifth earth angel.

3 p.m. I made my 3 p.m. flight.

4:30 p.m. I'm at the hospital. I gave Barry the sweet kiss that I wanted to give him by the end of the day, and he greeted me with a cute joke in return. "I guess the doctors gave me a Hawaiian Pineapple Stent."

7:00 p.m. The doctor wants to release him from the hospital as early as tomorrow.

January 22: One of the new heart medications caused serious side effects. He needs to stay here longer.

8:00 p.m. Jan just texted me. "This must be so hard for you, Melody. Write a letter to your "Shift of Heart" community. Tell them what's going on. Ask for their support." My friend is right. Learning to receive is as important as learning to give. I'll write a letter tonight.

January 23: We're finally in the hotel room together and I'm grateful to have him close to me again. There's still one problem. I can see that he's ill and my intuition tells me that what he's feeling isn't normal. Did they release him too soon? Should we stay at the hotel until he gets back on his feet? Should we go back to the hospital and have him reexamined?

Should we book a flight back to Massachusetts?

January 25: Believe it or not, we're on the plane. We decided to take a risk, book a flight, and head back to New England. As Dorothy from the *Wizard of Oz* said, "There's no place like home."

In Retrospect-The Healing Power of Love: *My fourteen hours on the plane allow me the luxury to reflect. During our crisis, I met one beautiful earth angel after another. Every single person in Kauai and Honolulu offered me their deep capacity for empathy and compassion. Every hotel clerk, waiter, taxi driver, nurse, doctor, nurse's aide, customer service representative and travel insurance agent showed heart-centered caring. Both airlines bent their strict cancelation rules and were guided by compassion. Everyone I met was led by pure love and kindness. They sure grow beautiful people in the land of paradise. Thank you, everyone. You gave me faith in humanity and in the healing power of love.*

January 25: Home Sweet Home.

In Retrospect-January 26: *Since we've been back, Barry has had a complication. No matter what, I will keep my faith, take all the ups and downs in stride, and learn to accept the ebb and flow of our new normal. This experience has given our relationship and life itself a fresh perspective. I value his every breath and savor each moment together. I know that we'll have a year of challenges, but I also know that these new days feel like rebirth and second chances. There is nothing like an emergency to shake things up. This is a sacred time to embrace new beginnings and to feel profound thankfulness.*

February 20: The other night we were talking about the healing power of words. In one second, Barry came up with eleven power words that will get us through all the hard times. Please use them in your own time of need too.

I have the strength and the will

to get past this.

Reaching Out

At any moment, we may be given the unexpected opportunity to become a healer and a light-worker for someone in need.

♥

My Letter: I swallowed my pride, reached out to the "Shift of Heart" community for help, and was greeted with a virtual circle of love, light, healing and strength…

January 22

Dear Community of Love,

This time it is me that needs your support. My husband and I went to Hawaii for a family vacation, and while we were there, our lives turned upside-down. There was one crisis after another. Our grandchildren were ill, there was a false missile threat, and my husband suffered a serious heart attack and had to be airlifted from Kauai to Honolulu. I would rather give to you than receive from you, but I am also desperate to breathe in any strength and positive energy that you can offer me. May I ask for a circle of love around me? Thank you, healers of light.

Gratefully,

Melody

Community Wisdom

*"If you realized how powerful your thoughts are,
you would never think a negative thought."*

Peace Pilgrim

After I wrote my letter, the "Shift of Heart" community uplifted my soul and nourished my spirit. Every member mirrored love, kindness and compassion with their caring heart and supportive words. If you find yourself needing more strength in your own life today, please breathe these words into your spirit. We are all one family of darkness and light and everyone requires support at times. Here are some of the healing messages that were sent my way...

This too shall pass. You are guided and loved all the way.

Gentle Healings, sweet sister.

You've got this because we've got you!

Remember to breathe! Be gentle with yourself.

May your journey help you to find the gifts in all of this.

Remember all those positive affirmations! Think positive!

Trust. Sending healing Angels.

Traveling the labyrinth with you in mind. People are sending you strength to keep your "well" full.

I send light bubbles of love and peace to your heart. Step by step, you'll get through it.

A Test of Fortitude

Just by imagining a better life,
you are already packed and on your way towards living it.

♥

When we are forced to deal with a sudden emergency, it feels as if we are living the story of Job from the Old Testament of the Bible. Our grief, exhaustion and fear torment us in the late hours of the night and distract us from feeling joy during the day. Life feels unfair and we think that everyone has it easier than we do. Although life's challenges are indeed a test of fortitude, let's give ourselves credit for all the times we came through with flying colors and stood tall in our resilience, determination, survival instincts, strength and courage.

How DO we do it? Isn't it amazing how many feelings dance with each other at the same exact time? Sadness AND joy. Anxiety AND courage. Each emotion dovetails or dances in parallel. How do we go through so many challenges and still feel a sense of sanity amid the insanity?

Right now, I am still concerned about my husband's health. Beneath the surface of "normal," I am anxious and worried. Despite these feelings, I have had many moments of laughter, managed to perform a concert, presented a motivational workshop at the library, watched the first hummingbirds sip nectar from the feeders, relaxed in the hammock while eating chocolate ice cream, watered the plants, fed the birds and worked on this book. Beneath these good moments, I still feel heavy undercurrents of anxiety and worry.

I know that I'm not alone. There may have been many times in your life when you were amazed by your own emotional flexibility too.

♥ **Life Wisdom:** The "ebb" parts of life are challenging, and as you can see, I teach what I need to learn. Let's make it a mutual intention to dance with the ebb and flow of life as gracefully as possible. Even during a crisis, focus on small moments of joy. Any positive distraction eases a heavy heart. Walk over to a colorful flower and let its beauty fill your soul. Look up at the sky and feel its promise. Close your eyes and listen to the call of each beautiful bird. Breathe in a beautiful piece of music that uplifts or calms you. Involve yourself in an activity that stabilizes your weary soul. Keep faith that this difficult time will pass. Reach out to family and friends, seek professional help and visualize a good outcome. Pray, cry, write, keep moving, meditate and take a slow sensory walk in nature. Open your heart to a stranger who needs a gentle smile, a listening heart and a soft place to fall. It can help remind you that other people are facing challenging situations too. Keep moving forward. Someone needs you now and someone will need you in the future. You are living through a test of fortitude and you are passing your test with flying colors. Believe in the magic of new moments. Just by imagining a better life, you are already packed and on your way towards living it. The world counts on your special resonance. Breath by breath, you have the power to climb out of the rabbit hole and step into a life of light, love and joy. Trust that your situation will shift for the better.

Put one foot in front of the other and walk the
path of hope, miracles and healing.

Paradise in Five Minutes

Here. Now. This.

♥

The following twelve gems will guide you towards inner paradise in less than five minutes…

Music: Music has always saved my life, my soul, my days and my moments. Play uplifting music. Conduct, sing, move, hum and whistle. It will shift your mood in less than a minute. If you're feeling sad, make up lyrics to your blues and sing them. Release your feelings of sadness, in tune or out of tune. If you want to feel more joy, let's hear your best "TA-DAA!" Breathe in the healing power of music. If you need calm and inner peace, choose music that soothes your spirit. If you need energy, choose music that makes your toes want to wiggle and your body want to dance. Then, do it!

Music is medicine without any negative side effects.

Movement: Add a favorite form of movement to your day. Keep your energy flowing. Even if you don't feel like doing any aerobic exercise today, put one foot in front of the other and walk at your own pace. Keep moving. If you're disabled, find a way to use your wheelchair, motorized scooter, crutches, walker or cane to support your desire to be *IN* the world.

Don't let anything stop you.

Nature: When I take a walk on my favorite trail, I notice all the sounds, smells, colors and shapes on the changing terrain. I am *in* my walk and it encompasses more than exercise. I am aware of my feet on the earth and I feel grounded and strong. As I look up at the sky, I breathe in hope and light. My heart feels a sense of gratitude for all of nature's beauty and I am delighted to flow with the exciting pulse of life.

Uplifting People: Surround yourself with a circle of people who are loving, empathic, compassionate, inspiring and supportive.

Breathe: Notice your breath. Inhale deeply. Exhale deeply. Enjoy the "beingness" of your breath and the beauty in *this* moment.

Self-Compassion: Discard any thoughts that don't encourage you to thrive. Don't allow self-hatred, self-judgment, inner put-downs, self-bullying or jealousy rule your life. Breathe in love, forgiveness, healing and compassionate understanding. If you find yourself dwelling on toxic thoughts about your past, present or future, return to the now of this moment. Here. Now. This.

The Stop Sign Technique: In the chapter, "Healing from Inside Out," I mentioned the stop sign technique. When you are in a negative whirlwind, visualize a big red stop sign with your loving face on it that says, "Stop fretting, dear one. Worry is a negative prayer. Snap out of it. Lift yourself up. Find a rainbow from the lessons in your life. Keep hope."

Get Lost in Another World: After we returned home from Hawaii, my husband needed to go back in the hospital. I came back to an empty home, my anxiety level was out of control again, and I didn't know how to make myself feel better. What did I do? I forced myself to write. Writing became a positive distraction and a gift of grounded stability. I don't know what I would have done without this book project. When I changed my focus, it reduced my anxiety and fed my soul. Writing became a meditation that helped me calm down. It was the only medicine I needed.

When you're in the middle of a challenging situation, change your focus too. Get lost in another world. Read inspirational quotations, walk in nature, or enjoy a quiet lunch with a good friend. Do anything that is beneficial to every cell of your body.

Visualization: Call on the power of your imagination. Visualize how you would *like* your life to unfold. *Live* your "best movie of the year."

The Healing Power of Words: Use all the examples in *Heart-Dreamer*. Change your life by changing your words.

Gratefulness: Remember to offer your personal "thank you" to the universe. Start a grateful journal. Look around and look within. It's the simple things in life that give us joy, a humble sense of gratitude and a renewed perspective in life.

Self-Love: Even if you find yourself struggling with low self-esteem, your self-love quotient may be higher than you realize. It took steadfast determination and survival skills to get you through many tough situations and you have chosen to honor your life, no matter what. Although your sense of self-esteem may require strengthening, you are well on your way towards loving yourself more every day.

Metta Meditation: Now that we've enjoyed higher vibrational activities, let's send our positive thoughts to all the people on our planet. Send each person the healing power of your love. Visualize peace.

A Poem for Peace

©Cheryl Melody Baskin
From the book, "Shift of Heart-Paths to Healing and Love"

Envision with me a shift of heart in all people who seek revenge.
A shift of heart on each side.
In those who hate and in those who are hated.

Imagine a day when those who have the power to destroy the world
Feel a transformational shift in their heart to save the world.

Search with me for all people to understand one another.
If we can't understand one another, may we at least, at the very least
Respect each of our differences.

Visualize sending a glorious beaming light
Through and around ourselves, each other and Mother Earth.
Let every living being suddenly feel love, transformation, celebration, tolerance and peace.

And may there be a shift of heart within all people of our small precious world.

I'm Still Here

(From the album, "Listen to the Whispers" by Cheryl Melody ©)

We are so much more than who we seem on the surface.

I'm still here
I'm still here
I'm still here
No matter what.

I am more than who I seem
More than meets the eye
More than who you know
No matter what.

Please shine the light inside me
Bring out the light inside me
See the light inside me
No matter what.

Take the time to know me
Take the time to see me
Take the time to love me
No matter what.

I am love
I am breath
And I'm still here
No matter what.

Chapter Eight

Follow Your Heart

Keep your heart open and your eyes up towards the light of hope.

It is never too late to notice the silver lining from your difficult experiences.

It is never too late to breathe in a new purpose, mission and dream.

A Listening Heart

I give my heart full permission to light my dreams.

My Magic Formula: I have a magic formula for living my one life. *I listen to my heart.* I also listen to my highest wisdom, third eye intuition, gut feeling, inner voice, left brain cognitive thoughts and my precious wisdom-whispers. Each component is a life compass wrapped into one holistic package. The heart and its other compatible friends guide our relationships, major and minor life decisions and big and small dreams. Give yourself enough uncluttered time and inner spaciousness to listen to that beautiful heart of yours.

Delusions of Grandeur: Heart-dreamers often ask themselves, "Should I *always* listen to my heart? What if it's wrong? Am I fooling myself? Do I have "delusions of grandeur?" The truth is that heart-dreamers *don't* always know the answers to their questions. They trust, listen to the whispers, open their heart, ask the universe for guidance, take risks, walk the light of their new dream, visualize a positive outcome, and notice how each action step feels deep within their soul.

Heart-Dreamers know everything without knowing anything.

Living in Alignment: In the chapter, "Secrets of a Heart-Dreamer," we thought about our core values. My core values are to spread the power of love, hope and peace wherever I go. If people and ideas align with my values, I welcome them into my life. I may not understand the rational reason why I am pursuing an unexpected path, but my mantra is trust and my highest wisdom is my guide. If something feels unsettling, I ask myself questions, weigh the pros and cons, and wait as long as it takes to become clear.

The Positive Energy of Fear: Do my fears stop me from moving ahead? It depends. There are times when I listen to my fears. They could be protecting me and telling me that something isn't quite right. I look within, take my time, and listen for those wonderful third eye wisdom-whispers. As soon as I realize that my fears have turned into excuses that prevent me from living my full potential, I take a leap of faith and move forward.

There are times when it is important to follow our heart because we are scared. Fear can be a positive energy force towards growth and opportunity. Remember. There are no wrong turns. Only different lessons.

An Unexpected Gift: Even if you are a die-hard realist and believe that dreams are impractical and unimportant, try to suspend that belief for ten minutes every day. Allow yourself the opportunity to daydream. Give that part of your spirit a little shake and sudden awakening. Open your heart and hear all the dream-whispers that call your name. Who knows? There may be a latent artist, inventor, writer or musician hiding deep inside your soul. Growth and opportunity can blossom at any age.

Can we MAKE our Dreams Come True? Yes. We can work hard, focus like an archer with a bow, hone our craft, make ourselves available for opportunities, say *YES* to the universe, visualize a positive outcome, and enjoy every single minute of our creative process.

There is also a less tangible element for "making" our dreams come true. Transformational comedian and author, Kyle Cease, offers a fresh perspective...

"Our job is to get out of the way of ourselves and let the art flow through us. We need to stop trying, stop doing and start allowing. We have no clue what we can be when we stop forcing and start being."

✴ **An Experiential Activity:** As you read the following questions, contemplate Kyle's philosophy, write in your journal and drop into your heart to hear custom-made answers.

- What does the deepest part of my soul need?

- How can I "stop trying so hard, stop doing so much, and start allowing the magic of life to happen?"

- Without forcing my dreams to manifest, what small action step can I take towards their actualization?

- What gives my heart a feeling of warmth and joy?

- Which limiting beliefs keep me from moving forward?

- If I visualized a better movie for my life, what would it look like?

Follow your Heart: Daydreaming and creativity helped me survive childhood bullying. I visualized a future that held promise and hope, and

I would spend long hours into the night creating stories and plays with themes of love and inclusion. As an adult, my healing has been rooted by writing songs and books that uplift the human spirit and unite us as one community of love.

All my dreams have been achieved by following my heart. I transformed my pain into my life's mission, purpose and work of love. You can too.

A Reason for Everything: Along the way, I discovered creative ways to cope with life's challenges and I also understand the silver lining behind most of my struggles. If you are wondering about the deeper meaning behind your own struggles, *trust*.

♥ **Life Wisdom:** Someday you will know your reason for everything. You will use your pain to help those in need, and by helping them, you will heal yourself. Your greater purpose will become your reason for everything. Always keep your heart open and your eyes up towards the light of promise and hope. It is never too late to notice the rainbow from your difficult experiences, and it is never too late to breathe in a new purpose, passion, mission and dream. Invite positive thoughts and people into your dynamic life, and when your dreams make themselves known, say *YES*. Walk towards the whispers, believe in yourself, move forward, and honor the meaning and purpose of your life. Don't lose sight of it for a minute. Even during difficult times, hold your dreams close to your heart and forge a unique path. Reach out with both wings, step into your butterfly spirit, and encourage your inner heart-dreamer to soar high. Believe. Dream. Listen. Do. Become. Trust. Love. Let go. Have fun.

There is only one beautiful you.

Shine in your uniqueness and design

an interesting life simply by being

who you are.

Blanket of Love

*There are times when we may need to invent an upside-down and
inside-out way to return to the soft place of love.*

I'm going to tell you about a marriage. Mine. We've been married for-ty-six years. When people hear how long we've been married, they are shocked. *"What's your secret? How DID you do it?"*

I could make up any number of witty answers, but I really don't know "how we did it." Marriage can be a challenge, and pressures, human sensitivities, generational patterns, traumatic life experiences, defensiveness and our wounds from childhood all influence the quality and the duration of a relationship. Personally, I think it is amazing that relationships work at all.

Despite our relationship of ups and downs, we are in love. We are also determined and deeply committed. We believe in the power of love, and we will do whatever it takes to make our love work. When my husband and I need marital help, we either seek counseling or participate in a relationship workshop. I'm the one who combs through a brochure and chooses just the right workshop on "how to give and receive love." You may be surprised to know that my husband usually does much better than me in these workshops. Once we're there, *he* is the one who is more enthusiastic.

Many years ago, we participated in a weekend workshop called "Marriage Encounter." The facilitators posted a large banner on the wall that said, "Love is a decision." The slogan confused me. I thought love was a feeling that only came from our heart. "Love is a decision" sounded much too logical. Despite my skepticism, I kept an open mind.

I really don't know that much about love. I'll just wait and see what the weekend offers.

It turns out that "love is a decision" was a powerful phrase after all. Long after the workshop ended, I used this affirmation time and time again. I would say, "Remember, Melody. Love is a decision." It became my mantra of hope.

Do you ever need to relearn some of life's lessons? Years later, we found ourselves struggling with our relationship again. During this challenging time, I decided to register for a relaxation workshop that focused on sound healing. The facilitator suggested that we bring a blanket. Once the participants were settled, our teacher asked us to lay down, cover ourselves with the blanket, and then close our eyes.

Allow the vibrations of the healing bowls enter each of your chakras. Breathe. Relax. Allow the sounds to heal you.

Easier said than done. I found it difficult to shake off my other feelings. Despite a strong resistance towards feeling a sense of inner peace, I decided to be an obedient student and give the workshop a good try. I reached for my blanket. As soon as it covered me, I felt a softening in my heart…

What was that? I'm still upset. Why did my heart just open?

Suddenly, I understood everything. My husband had given me the blanket as a gift. I know that a blanket may not seem like the most romantic present in the world, but it was a sweet gesture and it spoke volumes to me. He wanted me to know that he thought about me more than I realized. He just couldn't show his love "my way."

In a heightened moment of consciousness, I realized the depth of my husband's love. I reaffirmed the meaning of "love is a decision," and I slipped love back into my heart.

♥ **Life Wisdom:** We may not receive the exact words that we need to hear at the exact time we need to hear them. We may not receive the attention and cherishing that we deserve. Although it is always the goal to give and receive these qualities, it doesn't always happen that way in real life. While we are trying to sort out our own issues, it isn't always possible to show our partner how much we cherish them. Make it your intention to give and receive love, but also bend with its wind. Give each other the space to be imperfectly human. There is no cookie-cutter approach. There are times when we may need to invent an upside-down and inside-out way to return to the soft place of love.

Love may not always come to us in the way
that we want to define it.
Try anything that you can to get there. It's
worth it.

Doors

Become as curious as a toddler and as passionate as the sound of the cello. Once the timing is right, ZOOM! You're off and running!

♥

Doors are often viewed as a metaphor for opportunity or adversity. Let's focus on a closed door first. Some people believe that a closed door means that "it's over." It's time to look around for a different opportu-nity. Alexander Graham Bell said it best. "When one door closes, another opens."

♥ **Life Wisdom:** Although Alexander made an excellent point, there are more subtleties to a closed door than we may realize. If you are denied an opportunity, ask yourself questions. "What is this closed door saying to me? What lessons can I learn from it? Am I *sure* that this opportunity isn't "meant to be?"

Your highest wisdom will whisper custom-made answers.

What if the door is closed simply because of bad timing, fear, personal readiness, inner resistance or overwhelming anxiety? When your life aligns itself again, who knows? This very door may lead you to a life filled with magic and miracles.

Be patient. Some dreams take time.

While you are waiting for your dreams to actualize, they are constantly percolating within you. Once the right timing aligns itself with your passion and intention, ZOOM. You are off and running. If your heart still longs to step through this very door, you will hear a strong and persistent voice. When you least expect it, this door will open wide and say, "Come on in. I've been waiting for you. Welcome home."

Here's an idea. What if we don't need *any* doors to determine our destiny? What if doors, fences, boundaries and over-defined labels only inhibit growth and potential? Let's become as curious as a toddler and as passionate as the sound of a cello. The zing of life is rooted in life's open-ended possibilities.

You are the director, driver, captain and pilot of your destiny. It is up to you to make life happen.

Reach for the stars and enjoy all of life's delicious surprises. You have the power to create an endless flow of opportunities towards adventure, growth and change. Don't wait for doors to open or close. You know what you want. Make it happen.

Wherever your heart leads,

manifest a welcome sign!

Community Wisdom

"Welcome home. Step right through. You can do this."

The "Shift of Heart" community loved talking about doors as metaphors for adversity and opportunity. I had no idea that this subject could be so fascinating...

Patricia said that an open door depends on timing and alignment.

Thia respects the importance of deep inner curiosity and the fun of the journey. If a door closes, she always asks the universe for its lessons. What can she learn? Why is this door closed?

Debra feels that each person holds the right keys to the right doors.

Autumn was dealing with door replacements in her home and she was feeling extremely frustrated. She wondered what she was meant to learn from this home repair misery. She also agreed with me. Maybe she doesn't need any doors in her home or in her life.

Marilyn showed us a picture of all her newly painted doors. She had converted her plain white doors into colors that vibrated strong statements of strength, passion, creativity and beauty.

♥ **Life Wisdom:** Here's what I think. We need to do anything and everything to step towards our dreams. Open doors, close them, let go of them, climb through windows, slide down chimneys, stand on rooftops, don't take no for an answer, nod an affirmative YES to opportunities, and embrace multicolored doors that say, "Welcome home. Step right through. You can do this. You have everything that you need to become anything you want to be. Trust. Believe in yourself. Embrace the impossible and make it possible."

Paint your doors with the colors of love, courage, risk, faith, self-belief, joy, trust, strength, sparkle, excitement, glow, magic and optimism.

Elisabeth and Sonja

A true story of friendship, life, death, courage and love.

I first met Elisabeth and Sonja on vacation. They were best friends from Sweden, and because of their friendship and enthusiasm for life, they immediately touched my heart. I wanted to know more about them.

First, a little about Elisabeth...

Her joy was contagious and she was a glowing picture of radiant health. Her twinkling eyes, hearty laugh, gregarious personality and delight for living pulled me towards wanting to learn more about her and we immediately made a heart-centered connection. In short, Elisabeth was amazing.

She exuded magnetic sparkle and I was drawn towards her strong energy. I wanted to know her secret for living life so fully, and as we chatted, Elisabeth wasted no time. She told me that she had terminal cancer. She had three to six months to live. I was shocked. She didn't seem sick and she didn't look sick. Elisabeth challenged everything that I had assumed about dying, and I learned what it looks like to live with joy, *no matter what*.

And then there was Sonja...

It would be difficult to find a friend who never leaves your side during a time like this, but Sonja never left Elisabeth. As I witnessed the unconditional love that she offered her best friend, I was deeply honored to be around Sonja's beautiful soul. We became instant friends, and as I got to know her, I could also see that she was very deep and wise. After Elisabeth died, I asked her to share some of the deepest parts of herself. Sonja's wisdom moved me to tears…

I learned so much about living life through Elisabeth. I have had so much sorrow in my life, beginning when my dad died when I was only one-years-old. I have no tears left, but as I get older and wiser, I see that I need to just be present for each moment of each day. Elisabeth felt that I worried too much and encouraged me not to worry about things that may never happen.

I stayed with Elisabeth, because I followed my heart.

I stayed with friends and family members who were dying, because I followed my heart.

I stayed with my brother, because I followed my heart.

When people take me for granted, I do it anyways. I follow my heart.

There was a time when I didn't follow my heart when it came to men. I didn't choose well. I lived with someone who made me feel that I had to be perfect all the time. Perfect clothes, makeup and hair. Years later, I met Gerry. He makes me feel so loved compared to that other one. I followed my intuition when I met him, and I am so happy I did. With Gerry, I can wear clothes that are appropriate for playing with our dog, and I don't need to brush my hair or put on any makeup. What does he tell me anyway? "I'm good looking, I'm nice, I love you." It's true love. He sees my heart and not my face.

We must listen to what the "feeling power" tells us. Your first thought is usually right.

♥ **Life Wisdom:** Sonja is beautiful inside and out. No matter what she goes through, she follows her heart. The story about Elisabeth and Sonya is here to remind us about the beauty of unconditional love, following one's heart, friendship, deep listening, wisdom, ebb and flow, grace, gratefulness, surrender, emotional support, life, death, living each moment, determination, self-awareness, steadfast loyalty, dignity, hope, grief and joy.

Both friends changed my perspective on life and death, and I hope that their story of truth, courage, friendship and love touched you as well.

Follow your heart.

Humanity 101

How about a different kind of to-do list?

A Journal Writing Entry: I've been a turtle in a shell lately, and it's time to break out and make conscious changes. To make these changes, I've decided to create a different kind of to-do list. It's called "Humanity 101." By creating a more conscious way to live, love is always my common ground. Although there will always be many to-dos on my other list, "Humanity 101" will become my top priority everywhere I go and in everything I do.

A typical to-do list at a certain stage in life...

Pick up kids. *Check.* Bring them to soccer. *Check.* Go grocery shopping. *Check.* Get to the doctor's appointment on time. *Check.* Fix the car. *Check.* Answer emails. *Check.* Bring the baby to daycare. *Check.* Go to class. *Check.* Make dinner. *Check.* Go to work. *Check.* Have a heart-to-heart with my partner. *Check.* Read that book. *Check.* Sign the kids up for gymnastics, ballet and music. *Check.* Research schools. *Check.* Rehearse for the concert. *Check.* Bring my mom to the doctor. *Check.* Make phone calls. *Check.* Pick up two birthday cards. *Check.* Go to the meeting. *Check.* Bring the dog to the vets. *Check.* Exercise. *Check.* Clean up the yard. *Check.* Clean the house. *Check.*

Rat race alert! There is no time left to stop, look, listen, feel or breathe. "Humanity 101" returns me back to basics. It taps into the softer side of life...

My Humanity 101 List

- *Love.* Remember that all my paths lead to love.

- *Reach out.* Become a beacon of light, inspiration and hope.

- *Give.* Give without any expectations.

- *Good Vibes.* Aim for optimism. Wherever I go, spread the power of love.

- *Feel.* Keep my heart open.

- *Be.* Just breathe and be.

- *Backbone.* Stand in my truth.

- *Speak up.* Give myself an empowered voice. Step into my "Ta-Daa!"

- *Communicate.* Share my truth with clarity, strength and love.

- *Help.* Do whatever I can to help make the world a better place.

- *People.* Listen, uplift and inspire.

- *Forgive.* Open my heart towards the healing that forgiveness can bring. Whenever possible, forgive.

- *The Earth.* Honor and respect the earth's sensitivity and healing beauty.

- *Friendship.* Be a good friend to myself. Be a good friend to others.

- *Awaken.* Stay awake, aware, conscious and fully present.

- *Stay Open.* Give people a chance. Learn from people who are different from me.

- *Visualize.* Picture my life as I would like it to be. Picture the world as I would like it to be. Believe.

- *Align.* Align myself with love.

- *Hope.* Always keep it. Always give it to others.

- *Peace.* Visualize peace within and peace on our planet.

- *Trust.* Trust that the universe is working *with* me. There is a higher reason for everything.

- *Keep Moving.* Put one foot in front of the other. Keep moving forward. I don't need to know where I'm going. I just need to trust.

- *Laugh.* It's healing.

- *Naps.* When needed, take them.

- *Believe in myself.* I can do it.

- *Remember.* I am enough. Life is enough.

- *Risk.* Be courageous. Step into the unknown mystery of life, love, creativity and dreams.

- *Focus.* Focus on the positive pulse of life.

- *Wisdom-Whispers.* Listen for them. Pay attention.

- *Heart-Dreamer.* Remember that my dreams and my heart are always connected.

- *Follow.* Follow the whispers of my heart.

Community Wisdom

I asked the "Shift of Heart" community...

"If you could share one big or small lesson from our school called "Life 101," what would it be?"

Dr. Bernie Siegel, MD: "As a physician, I have seen so-called incurable patients be cured when they accepted their death, went home, and started living what their heart wanted them to live. One patient went off to the beautiful mountains of Colorado to die. A year later, I called to ask why I wasn't invited to the funeral, and he said, "It was so beautiful here, I forgot to die." Another patient wrote me that she let her heart take over her life and did many things, including getting a dog. Her letter ended with, "I didn't die, and now I'm so busy, I'm killing myself." Where do I go from here? My answer was for her to take a nap. On her fridge, one woman put, "When you live in your heart, magic happens," and her AIDS healed."

Mala: "I think the heart is like a signature frequency...and no matter what...the sickness...the dark times...the falls...the disappointments... this is the only space that rings true...like...I KNOW ...without a doubt who I am…and my heart is the closest place where I can expand it…be it…feel it."

Lorie: "Trust with certainty that things will work out and you will be guided."

Betsy: "True joy comes from service to others, and in being grateful for all you have."

Elisabeth: "Sorry if my English is not okay. I am from Sweden. I am 53 years old and have lived a great life, always enjoying my day. Now I have Ovarian cancer stage 4B, but I still enjoy life. You always have a choice. A: To enjoy life. B: To be scared of life."

Pat: "I have learned late in life to follow my initial gut instinct. It's always right."

Maggie: "I have a pink "food for thought" processor! It has no blades, but it does stir things up quite a bit. I put all my worries and concerns into it with some cream and sugar, and then I start it up and listen to the little motor as it whirrs! Of course, this is a mind game, but an effective one. If you visualize this new movie, instead of harping on what's worrisome, you'll reap the sweet surprise of some peace of mind!"

Cynthia: "I truly believe that everyone can explore happiness in their life and bring it to their own path. Happiness is a choice. My choice is to spread joy and inspire people to see the world with their eyes full of love!"

Shelley: "Stay adventurous and embrace life to the fullest!"

Autumn: "Drama isn't worth it. Just chill."

Mary-Jane: "This too shall pass" is my mantra in the school of life. Have patience, take a deep breath, and know that time tends to lessen most pain. We are all in the need of healing. We need to use our strength and love to make this world a more peaceful and caring place. I'm committed to showing others love, not anger. Confidence, not fear. Mercy, not revenge."

Jean: "I know that everything happens for a reason. I ask myself, "What are the lessons that I'm supposed to be learning?" Then, I listen."

Sue: "Never give up! Tomorrow always brings new simple joys. Get up and get going!"

Rebecca: "I continually circle back to the journey. I offer my gratitude and maintain my faith."

Lana: "Author, Carolyn Myss, often talks about the transformational power of *"Grace."* Grace teaches me that I have a choice on how I respond to negative or uninformed statements from well-meaning people. Even when my ego would like to "let them have it" or correct them, I can extend mercy and forgiveness from my heart. When my mother, who has dementia, continually asks me the same questions over and over within ten minutes, "grace" helps me extend compassion and patience. When people tell me how to run my life in any given situation, or who to vote for or what to do, "grace" reminds me to stay in a place of love and to live and let live. It transforms judgmentalism and the need to be right to a place of peace, love, respect and tolerance."

Colette: "Find what you love and keep on climbing!"

Lisa: "Trust. In quiet meditation, I love to go near water. It always centers me. I especially love finding beautiful seashells. I feel positive energy from all the different colors of the shells. It's kind of like following the colors of the chakras!"

Paula: "I try to be the best that I can be each day. I feel such gratefulness and love when I see a beautiful smile of a child, a senior citizen couple holding hands, the salt air of the sea, or my children laughing on the couch reminiscing about their baby pictures. Life should never be taken for granted. It is magnificent. We should focus on all we DO have, and not on what we don't have. I work with a student who survived the Rwanda Genocide in 2004. She also traumatically watched her father and brother get massacred in front of her. She comes to school every day to educate herself, stay strong and to never give up. She changed my life and has given me more than she will ever understand."

Thia: "Faith in the Universal energy. If you don't have faith, fear will enter. Love yourself. I find that when I am clear about what my heart wants, I have no fear. The worst part is when other people express their fears about what I am doing. It doesn't help me in any way. It creates a lack of confidence and doubt. All I need is one thing. My heart! When I follow my heart, everything is magical. I get all the help I need, and everything falls into place."

Cecilia: "Be authentic and genuine. "Do unto others as you want others do unto you." Find people with the same vibrational frequency as you. Go out for walks, observe nature at work and people watch."

Shelly: "Honor the energy and being that is present within you every moment of the day. Embracing it will take you to places that you never imagined."

Nancy: "I was in very high spirits this afternoon. I realized that I felt that way because I helped a few friends that needed me. I got over myself and gave to someone else."

Naomi: "I have learned to listen to my inner voice. It helped me release someone that wasn't meant for me or good for my well-being. It made me take a positive step forward with my life."

Candice: "Stand together in love."

Joan: "As I do my morning chores, I like to sing and dance all by myself. My cats seem to like it too. I walk in the woods as often as I can, and I take the time to visit the water there. I lean back on a nice tree to feel its calm and quiet strength, and then I sit and listen to the sweetest sound of all-the songs of the birds."

Ann: "I send heart energy to myself and to others."

Janet: "Sometimes when I'm down on myself, I'll say wildly exaggerated things to myself. It can just be a fun, whimsical thing. I've been reading that our brain believes what we tell it, so why not say to yourself, "You're so amazing!" "Wow, you're doing a fabulous job with that!" Just give yourself a boost."

Dru: "I create a slow day with lots of rest, and I surround myself with the things I love-flowers, spiritual music, books and my paints."

Tonya: "I may have saved a few marriages. A few of my girlfriends were complaining about their husbands and thinking about divorcing them. I asked them, "If you woke up tomorrow and he was gone, how would you feel if there were no more conversations, no last question, and no more hugs or kisses. He was just gone. They said, "I couldn't live with that." Life changes in a second. Don't be foolish. This person knows you better than anyone. They have been your best friend and they made you feel safe. You're always stronger together than apart."

John: "Pay attention to your beliefs, because you actually believe what you believe and act upon it, whether it is true or untrue, healthy or unhealthy, rational or irrational."

Steven: "I try to be only interested in what's going on with others without mentioning my own stuff. Smile. Meditate. Say, "In this moment, may all be well.""

Debbie: "I love this quote by Thich Nhat Hanh. *With mindfulness, you can recognize the presence of the suffering in you and in the world, and it's with that same energy that you tenderly embrace the suffering.* It makes me cry with its profound truth."

Librada: "When I think of the word "peace," I think of the creek nearby and how much peace it gives me."

Susan F: "Our mutual friend knew that peace begins with the children. I always think of Janet when I think of peace, and I try to live by her motto, "peace begins with me.""

Matt: "Keep music in your life! I especially love a guitar piece called "By Candlelight" by Andrew York. I find healing in his music, and I allow the sounds of his music wash over me as I listen."

Laurel: "Think positive that everything will be okay. Believe!"

Renee: "Let go and let God (Spirit, Universe, Love)."

Jan: "Dance, dance, dance! It's good for the body and soul! I love to dance with other people. It's great to be in a crowd of happy people who are grooving to the music. It makes me feel so happy."

Eden: "When life feels at its worst-scary, lonely and very dark-think of what means the most to you and hang onto that thought. If you hang on really really tight, you will have the strength to hang on until the light slowly returns or until you discover a path out of the situation you find yourself in. It does get better."

Perla: "Dreams awaken us to survive in this world. They make us look up for the big things in life. Without them, we are nothing. Dreams give us the strength to keep fighting for happiness."

The Real Winner

When you find just the right place and just the right fit for your passion, your heart will sing forever.

♥

Roll out the red carpet! Are you ready for your golden trophy? Your "Life Achievement Award" is here to acknowledge your growth and potential as a starry-eyed dreamer and a doer of big dreams. It is also here to recognize your persistent determination, resilience, courage and strength. The whole world celebrates you today. Receive the positive energy and breathe it into your soul. You deserve the accolades. Despite life's challenges, you chose to honor your inner heart-dreamer.

Look! A standing ovation. Rise. Stand in the glow. Take a confident bow. Hear the applause? See the beaming faces? Feel all the support and love? The gong rings and the trumpets resound for you, my friend, just for you. The whole world honors you.

We are positively impacted and inspired because YOU are here.

Congratulations. You have officially stepped into the spirit of a heart-dreamer. You look up at the stars with dreams in your eyes, trust in the magical mystery of the unknown, honor your truth, and embrace your life with love, courage and curiosity.

What resilience! Grit! Flame! Passion! Fire in your belly!

Look! More cheering, confetti, bubbles, trumpets, singing bowls, magic wands of golden light, gongs, kazoos and balloons! They are all here for *you*. Stand in your light, dear one, and stand proudly.

All of life vibrates, "Thank You!"

- ♥ *Thank you* for being here.

- ♥ *Thank you* for being a light-worker.

- ♥ *Thank you* for your open and listening heart.

- ♥ *Thank you* for being an inspiration.

- ♥ *Thank you* for offering empathy and kindness to others.

- ♥ *Thank you* for your ability to show compassion and love.

- ♥ *Thank you* for keeping an open mind.

- ♥ *Thank you* for sharing your vulnerability.

- ♥ *Thank you* for sharing your strength.

- ♥ *Thank you* for your generosity.

- ♥ *Thank you* for your open spirit.

♥ *Thank you* for honoring your highest intuition.

♥ *Thank you* for living from a place of love.

♥ *Thank you* for being your own best friend.

♥ *Thank you* for choosing to be a supportive and loving friend to others.

♥ *Thank you* for being curious about life.

♥ *Thank you* for your spirit of adventure.

♥ *Thank you* for believing in the mystical magic of the unknown.

♥ *Thank you* taking a leap of faith and betting on yourself all the way.

♥ *Thank you* for knowing that you are enough just as you are.

♥ *Thank you* for changing your life by changing your words.

♥ *Thank you* for just being and breathing.

♥ *Thank you* for keeping your eyes focused on hope, promise and light.

♥ *Thank you* for taking conscious steps to honor our one earth.

♥ *Thank you* for living the path of love as the *truest* meaning of success.

♥ *Thank you* for giving yourself life coaching pep talks.

♥ *Thank you* for listening to your wise inner guru.

♥ *Thank you* for stepping into your strengths.

♥ *Thank you* for acknowledging your many talents.

♥ *Thank you* for never giving up and always moving forward.

♥ *Thank you* for doing the inner work that it takes to grow, change and heal.

♥ *Thank you* for taking yourself as lightly as the angels do.

♥ *Thank you* for listening to your inner voice.

♥ *Thank you* for paying attention to your wisdom-whispers.

♥ *Thank you* for always believing that anything and everything is possible.

♥ *Thank you* for honoring your rich memoir as your story of inspiration.

♥ *Thank you* for offering your wisdom as your greatest gift.

♥ *Thank you* for believing in the healing power of love.

♥ *Thank you* for saying YES to every opportunity that the universe offers.

♥ *Thank you* for honoring the passion of your dreams.

♥ *Thank you* for trusting uncertainty.

♥ *Thank you* for showing up for yourself.

♥ *Thank you* for showing up for others.

♥ *Thank you* for making each person feel that they matter.

♥ *Thank you* for stepping into your full potential.

♥ *Thank you* for visualizing hope.

♥ *Thank you* for trusting in the flowing river of life.

♥ *Thank you* for being an earth angel to someone in their time of need.

♥ *Thank you* for being love, shining love and standing in love.

♥ *Thank you* for realizing that every moment is a new beginning.

♥ *Thank you* for acknowledging all the little things that create happiness.

♥ *Thank you* for dancing with the ebb and flow of life.

♥ *Thank you* for visualizing peace.

♥ *Thank you* for sharing your truth with others so that they will be inspired to share their truth too.

♥ *Thank you* for being willing to explore and discover who you are.

♥ *Thank you* for bringing your magic wand of golden light everywhere you go.

♥ *Thank you* for making a difference in the world.

♥ *Thank you* for daydreaming.

♥ *Thank you* for being open to a never-ending flow of creativity.

♥ *Thank you* for making the world a softer place.

♥ *Thank you* for not allowing perfection and fear stand in the way of your dreams.

♥ *Thank you* for daring to dream bigger dreams today than you did yesterday.

♥ *Thank you* for believing in the dreamer inside you.

♥ *Thank you* for listening to the songs in your heart.

♥ *Thank you* for stepping into your butterfly spirit.

♥ *Thank you* for joining our amazing community of heart-dreamers.

We open our hearts to your magnificence. Stand in your light, dear one. Love and accept all the perfectly imperfect parts of yourself. Water the seeds of your delicate soul with love and compassionate understanding and remember that every moment is an opportunity for rebirth and hope. Sing your award-winning original songs of dreams, fairy dust, miracles, magic, mystery, courage, risk, starlight, rainbows and wishing stars.

It is time to stand on top of our metaphorical mountain and shout with joy...

I am a heart-dreamer! I stand here with my arms open to all of life's unlimited possibilities! I dream. I act upon my dreams. I love. I am loved. I honor the truth of who I am. I follow the whispers of my heart and walk towards life, love, creativity and dreams, no matter what!

Follow Your Heart

(From the album, "Listen to the Whispers" by Cheryl Melody ©)

When you've lost your way, listen to your heart. It knows the truth.

♥

It's a simple song of living, I know just what to do
Follow your heart, let it lead you
Let your heart be your guide every single day
Let it shine a light all along your way.

Follow your bliss, follow the light
What do you want? It will be alright
Look for the warmth that you feel inside
Follow your heart with your arms open wide.

What is your purpose? What feels so good?
Don't live your life with wish and should
Follow the path that's unique to you
Follow your heart in what you feel and do.

It's a simple song of living, I know just what to do
Follow your heart, let it lead you
Let your heart be your guide every single day
Let it shine a light all along your way.

One More Thing

What inspirational messages will YOU leave behind?

Every quotation in this book of love and dreams was chosen for a special reason. Words are powerful. I wanted to surround your inner heart-dreamer with each word's positive vibration. I also wanted the dreams of the people who created these words travel into the soul of your own dreams.

There are quotations in here by authors, poets, teachers, spiritual leaders, psychologists, creative arts specialists, storytellers, a transformational comedian, artists, innovative doctors, environmental activists, peace and justice advocates, educators, philosophers, scientists, public speakers, actors, visionaries, television hosts, journalists, political commentators, human rights activists, musicians and mystics.

Allow their dreams to be the energy that honors your own dreams. Allow their inspiration to seep into your soul.

One more thing. If you could share your own pearls of wisdom from "Life 101," what messages would you leave behind? What would you say to uplift and inspire others to live a life of joy, light, optimism, courage, determination and unending dreams? Who knows? Someone may want to use *your* quote in their book someday.

Above all, thank you. Thank you for going on this journey with me. I needed the company.

From one heart-dreamer to another,

Melody

A Special Acknowledgment

"Eagle Eye," *Heart- Dreamer* and Me

Because of his keen eye for detail, I like to call him, "Eagle Eye." His real name is Barry Rosenbloom and he is my husband. When *Heart-Dreamer* was in its embryonic stage and at its completion, he helped me with editing and offered his fresh perspective. Due to our close relationship, my fierce independence and his tendency to be blunt, our process could have gone badly. It didn't. In fact, it was magical. He was sensitive to my feelings, truthful about his insights, and respectful of my work. As a result, we became closer and saw each other with new eyes.

Heart-Dreamer was graced by love. It is as if Glenda, the good witch from *The Wizard of Oz*, waved her magic wand around both of us. After forty-six years, we learned once again that love can grow in random and unexpected ways. This book had our love surrounding it and I hope that you can feel that love coming towards your own heart as well.

Barry, thank you for your time, unique perceptions, support, sensitivity and attention to detail. Thank you for coming closer when I needed it and backing off when I needed it too. I will always cherish working on "Heart-Dreamer" with you in my heart.

With a Grateful Heart

Shift of Heart Community - Writing a book is a solo journey, but I felt your circle of love around *Heart-Dreamer* every step of the way. Even though "I am old and wise," I didn't want to be the only voice in this book. Wisdom has no age, and I wanted the world to hear your wisdom too. By sharing your life experiences and insights, you grew into a village of inspiration for others. Thank you for your participation and for uplifting the vibration of the world towards peace, love and healing.

Judes Look Why - Thank you for sharing your beautiful poem with the world. The words in "Ode to Me" serve to remind all of us to love, respect and nurture ourselves more each day. Your constant depth of wisdom and quest to grow, heal and love are inspirational, and it is such an honor to have you in my life. I still remember the day we met. After I performed, you were the only person who offered to help carry my equipment and props back to my car. In that one shining moment, I knew that I had just found a special human being and a new friend.

Sonja Dahlgren - Thank you for giving me permission to share the story about your precious friendship with Elisabeth and for all your personal stories that encourage us to follow our heart. You have taught me so much about the power of unconditional love.

Elisabeth Bruhn - Although you have left our planet, thank you for teaching me about living and loving while dying. Your message and beautiful spirit lives on.

Ricky Kej - Thank you. Despite all your global concerts to raise human consciousness about the state of our environment, you somehow managed to read *Heart-Dreamer* and write a stellar testimonial on its behalf. When I think of a "heart-dreamer," I think of you. "You look up at the stars with dreams in your eyes, trust in the magical mystery of the unknown, honor your truth, and embrace your life with love and courage." One day you are doing a concert on behalf of the United Nations at the Palace of the Nations in Geneva, Switzerland. The next week you are performing for a conference with a theme of air pollution. The next month, you are in Chennai, India performing for 7000 people. In between, you somehow kept your word and read *Heart-Dreamer*. I am grateful to you beyond all words.

Dr. Bernie Siegel - Bernie, it is such an honor to have your positive vibration in *Heart-Dreamer* and I am touched that we connected in such a personal way. I have had the honor of reading your books for many years and have always been inspired by your innovative healing approaches, spiritual teachings and generous spirit. Thank you for offering to write a beautiful testimonial. I also want to tell you how much I appreciate your interest in *Heart-Dreamer*. I've always wanted a Fairy Godmother. It looks like I found a Fairy Godfather who knows how to spread magic, healing, support and miracles everywhere he goes.

Reverend Dr. Debbie Clark - Saying thank you seems insufficient. It was 1:30 in the morning when I received your beautiful testimonial and your words were like a soothing massage to my weary soul. Your open spirit and loving heart are a light amid the chaos in the world. When I wrote the section on earth angels, I was thinking of you. Thank you for your advocacy towards peace, inclusion and love. I am always inspired by the way you bring people from every walk of life back to the purity of loving each other with one heart.

Elisa Pearmain - In the middle of your rich and busy life, you said yes. Thank you for your beautiful testimonial. Years ago, we sat together in a creative arts class in college and I knew then that you were a very special human being. I also had an intuitive feeling that our paths would connect in the future. Here we are and I'm sure that this is only the beginning. Thank you for your wisdom and loving heart. I am so pleased that your special vibration is in here. I also want you to know how much I have always appreciated your creativity, your gift for storytelling, and your ability to offer an open and listening heart to others.

Ann Marie Speicher - Every time I walked into the library and parked myself in a chair to write for the day, you were my friendly and supportive light. Thank you for reading the many drafts of my book and for your positive comments and editing expertise as well. It takes tremendous self-belief to write a book and I admit that I found myself wavering at times. Your positive comments meant so much to me at just the right time. It was food for my soul, and it kept me going. It took courage to show you a draft of my book, and I chose just the right person. Thank you for everything, including the side-benefit of a new friendship.

Alan O'Hare - I have always valued your never-ending creativity and gift for storytelling, and I am delighted that you are part of the vibration in *Heart-Dreamer*. Thank you for the thought and energy that you brought to writing your testimonial and for even agreeing to do it. I know what a busy schedule you keep. Because a large part of this book is about creativity and dreams, Alan O'Hare just had to grace its pages. Thank you for all that you do to help people tell their honest life stories without any fear of judgment.

Dot Walsh - Where do I begin? You bring such light and love to the world. A line in *Heart-Dreamer* reminds me of you: "Be love, shine love and stand for love." The words reflect your special essence, Dot. I deeply appreciate your activism towards the actualization of peace, justice, love, faith and healing. Thank you for all that you do to help make the world a more loving place and thank you for being part of the vibration of this book of love and light.

Irene Hannigan - Thank you for giving me your permission to quote your own wonderful book, and most of all, thank you for all your support and wisdom along the way. The best class that I ever took was when I walked into your wonderful writing workshop and it resulted in a loving and magical friendship. In *Heart-Dreamer*, I talk about the importance of a friendship that is based on love, compassion and support. I am honored to say that our friendship mirrors it all. Here's to many more dynamic lunches of honest reflection, laughter, love, creative brainstorming and never-ending dreams.

Kristine Rencs - Thank you for your open and loving heart and for your design expertise that gifted the pages of *Heart-Dreamer*. You saved my dream my friend and I will always appreciate it beyond all words.

Shannon Matos - Thank you for your expertise and calming personality. I was initially nervous to have my picture taken, but as soon as I met you, it became a transformational spiritual experience.
www.shannonmatosphotography.com

Permissions

Sincere gratitude to all those who generously gave me their permission to include their words in *Heart-Dreamer*.

- Fred Rogers. Creator and host of "Mr. Rogers' Neighborhood," musician and minister. (Quote by Fred Rogers provided courtesy of the Fred Rogers Company). www.fredrogers.org
- Dr. Bernie Siegel, MD. Physician, spiritual teacher, and author of *365 Prescriptions for the Soul* and *Love, Medicine and Miracles*. www.berniesiegelmd.com
- Brené Brown, PhD, LMSW. Research professor, University of Houston; author of *Dare to Lead* and *The Gifts of Imperfection*. www.brenebrown.com
- Ram Dass. Spiritual teacher and author of *Be Here Now*. www.RamDass.org
- Marianne Williamson. Spiritual leader and author of *A Return to Love*. www.marianne.com
- Leo Buscaglia. Author, professor, speaker. CITATION. Reprinted from permission of SLACK Incorporated. *Living, Loving & Learning*. Thorofare, NJ. Slack, Incorporated, 1982.
- Sarah Ban Breathnach. Author of *Simple Abundance: A Daybook of Comfort and Joy* and *Something More: Excavating your Authentic Self*. www.sarahbanbreathnach.com
- Anne Lamott. Author of *Bird by Bird: Instructions on Writing and Life*. Novelist, non-fiction writer, political activist, public speaker, writing teacher. www.instagram.com/annelamott
- Dr. Geraldine Schwartz. Educator, psychologist, applied scientist and poet. Author of *Journeys of Second Adulthood*. www.thevisioneers.ca
- His Holiness the Dali Lama. Spiritual leader. www.dalailama.com

- Thich Nhat Hanh. Quotation reprinted from *No Mud No Lotus: The Art of Transforming Suffering* (2014) by Thich Nhat Hanh with permission of Parallax Press, Berkeley, California. www.parallax.org
- Tama Kieves. Inspirational coach and speaker. Author of *This Time I Dance! Trusting the Journey of Creating the Work You Love* and *Inspired and Unstoppable-Wildly Succeeding in Your Life's Work.* www.tamakieves.com
- David Whyte. Poet and author of *The Heart Aroused: Poetry and the Preservation of the Soul in Corporate America.* www.davidwhyte.com
- Rabbi Natan Segal. Spiritual leader and musician. *"From You I Receive."* www.natan.net
- Kyle Cease. Transformational comedian, speaker and author of *I Hope I Screw This Up: How Falling in Love with Your Fears Can Change the World.* www.kylecease.com
- Bill Moyers. Journalist and political commentator. www.billmoyers.com
- Irene Hannigan. Author of *Write On! How to Make Writing A Pleasurable Pastime.* www.facebook.com/writeonirenehannigan
- Malala Yousafzai. Activist and youngest Nobel Prize laureate. www.malala.org
- Dana Claudat. Feng Shui expert. www.fengshuidana.com
- Andrew York. Grammy award winning classical guitarist and composer. www.andrewyork.net
- Peace Pilgrim. Spiritual teacher and peace activist. www.peacepilgrim.org

About the Author

Cheryl Melody Baskin, (also known as "Melody"), is an award-winning author, playwright, musician, intuitive life coach, peace and spirituality educator, motivational speaker and sound healer.

Her inspirational books and plays include *Peace Dreamer: A Journey of Hope in Bad Times and Good, Heart-Dreamer: Stepping into Life, Love, Creativity and Dreams - No Matter What, Shift of Heart: Paths to Healing and Love,* and *Peace Begins with You and Me - A Musical Play with Life-Changing Messages for Every Generation.*

As a musician, she is a performing artist and has nine award-winning albums with positive messages for both adults and children. She is also the founder, moderator and intuitive life coach of "Shift of Heart," a large and inclusive Facebook community of love, peace, support and hope.

"Melody" enjoys a balance of quiet contemplation, meaningful social interaction, dreaming new dreams, and the healing power of nature. She is also a strong believer in peace, diversity celebration, listening to life's wisdom whispers, trusting in the magical mystery of the unknown, healing from inside-out, and walking the path of love.

Cheryl Melody Baskin was recently honored with a Lifetime Achievement Award from The Visioneers International Network.

Contact Information

CHERYL MELODY BASKIN

Official Website:
www.cherylmelody.com

Email: cherylmelody@gmail.com

Come Join Us! Shift of Heart Facebook Global Community of support, healing, inclusion and love:
https://www.facebook.com/groups/103850356767217/

"Cheryl Melody's" Music:
www.cherylmelody.com
Songs and albums by Cheryl Melody can be purchased on iTunes and on any streaming service.

Books:

**Peace Dreamer: A Journey of Hope
in Bad Times and Good**

**Heart-Dreamer: Stepping into Life,
Love, Creativity and Dreams-No Matter What
(Second Edition)**

Shift of Heart-Paths to Healing and Love

Peace Begins with You and Me-School Musical

Music and Books © Cheryl Melody Baskin, LLC

Made in the USA
Middletown, DE
22 May 2022

65995912R00149